Song of the Andes

David Miller, an American, has lived in Bolivia since 1981, working as a missionary with the Church of God. An itinerant evangelist and Bible teacher among the indigenous Andean peoples, he also freelances for various Christian news agencies. David and his wife, Barbara, are the parents of four children.

Also by David Miller:

The Lord of Bellavista
The Story of a Prison Transformed
(Triangle 1998)

The Path and the Peacemakers
The Triumph over Terrorism of the Church in Peru
(Triangle 2001)

Song of the Andes

The Impact of the Gospel on the Andean Peoples of Bolivia

DAVID MILLER

For you shall go out in joy,
and be led forth in peace;
the mountains and the hills before you
shall break forth into singing.
(Isaiah 55.12a)

TRIANGLE

Published in Great Britain in 2002 by
Triangle
SPCK
Holy Trinity Church
Marylebone Road
London NW1 4DU

First published in Spanish in 1992 by Los Amigos del Libro,
Cochabamba, Bolivia.

British Library Cataloguing-in-Publication Data

A catalogue record for this book is available from the British Library

ISBN 0-281-05466-5

Typeset by Trinity Typing, Wark-on-Tweed
Printed in Great Britain by Omnia Books, Glasgow

To Homer and Elvira Firestone,
two good and faithful servants.

Contents

Acknowledgements

I want to express my thanks to Florencio and Julia Colque for the many hours they spent with me recalling the history included in this narrative. Froilan and Angel Colque also contributed unique, personal testimony. Dr Homer Firestone and Mrs Elvira Firestone shared openly about their long missionary career in Bolivia and helped edit chapters 6 and 8. Dr Ronald Firestone gave valuable assistance in this aspect as well. I am indebted to Dr Donald Brockington and his wife, Dr Lolita Brockington, who together form a gifted research team, for their helpful insights into Bolivian history.

Without the patient counsel of these good people, this book could not have been written.

List of Characters

Atahualpa, Inca. Last ruler of the Inca empire. Subdued and executed by Francisco Pizarro.

Charles I of Spain and V of Austria, 1500–58. Holy Roman Emperor and King of Spain who commissioned the conquest of Peru.

Colque, Abel. Third son of Florencio and Julia Colque.

Colque, Angel. Eldest son of Máximo and Justina Colque, stepbrother to Florencio and Máxima Colque.

Colque, Asencio. Second son of Máximo and Justina Colque, stepbrother to Florencio Colque.

Colque, Casmiro. Florencio Colque's uncle and father of Froilan, Cresencio and Eulogio.

Colque, Cresencio. Second son of Casmiro Colque and first cousin of Florencio Colque.

Colque, Dionisio. Father of Máximo Colque and companion to Florencio on llama treks.

Colque, Eulogio. Youngest son of Casmiro Colque and first cousin of Florencio Colque.

Colque, Flora. Daughter of Máximo Colque and Valentina Vallejos Colque. Half-sister of Florencio and Máxima Colque.

Colque, Florencio. Son of Gregorio Colque and Valentina Vallejos Colque. Born in Lequepalca c.1937.

Colque, Froilan. Eldest son of Casmiro Colque and first cousin of Florencio Colque.

Colque, Gregorio. Father of Florencio Colque. Died in epidemic *c.*1940.

Colque, Isabel Leon. Wife of Angel Colque.

Colque, Javier. Youngest son of Florencio and Julia Colque.

Colque, Jonás. Second son of Florencio and Julia Colque.

Colque, José. Eldest son of Florencio and Julia Colque. Died in infancy.

Colque, Juan. Son of Máximo Colque and Valentina Vallejos Colque. Half-brother of Florencio and Máxima Colque.

Colque, Julia Leon. Wife of Florencio Colque and mother of José, Jonás, Abel and Javier.

Colque, Justina Vallejos. Sister of Valentina Vallejos and first wife of Máximo Colque. Died in childbirth.

Colque, Máxima. Sister of Florencio Colque. Died of tuberculosis at age 15.

Colque, Máximo. Widowed husband of Justina Vallejos, later married Valentina Vallejos Colque. Father of Angel, Asencio, Pablo and Juan.

Colque, Pablo. Youngest son of Máximo and Justina Colque. Mother died giving birth to him.

Colque, Valentina Vallejos. Mother of Florencio, Máxima and Juan.

Conde, Alberto. Aymara-speaking grocery merchant from Oruro. Founded the Association of Evangelical Congregations with Cirilo López.

Condori, Casiano. Farmer from Calapata who accepted Christ after his wife's healing.

Condori, Florencia Ramos. Wife of Casiano. Experienced healing that led to her family's acceptance of Christ.

Condori, Luciano. Aymara-speaking evangelist from La Paz who introduced the Firestones to Cirilo López and Alberto Conde.

de Toledo, Francisco. Viceroy of Peru from 1569 to 1581.

de Valverde, Vicente. Dominican friar who accompanied Francisco Pizarro on his expedition to overthrow the Inca empire. Later elected Bishop of Cuzco.

Doña Consuelo (alias). Originally from Chile. Owned first brothel on Cañada Strongest Street.

Estevez, Erasmo. Resident of Cañada Strongest Street who fought for removal of the brothels from the neighbourhood.

Firestone, Elvira Englund. Missionary and licensed nurse who served in Bolivia 1946 to present. Wife of Homer Firestone and mother of LeTaye and Ronald.

Firestone, Homer. Missionary and anthropologist who served in Bolivia 1946 until his death in 1996. Married to Elvira Englund.

Firestone, LeTaye. Chiropractor. Daughter of Homer and Elvira Firestone.

Firestone, Ronald. Chiropractor and pastor. Son of Homer and Elvira Firestone.

Huáscar, Inca. Assumed throne of the Inca empire upon the death of Huayna Kapac, but defeated in a civil war 8 years later by his brother Atahualpa and deposed.

Huayna Kapac, Inca. Last undisputed ruler of the Inca empire. Died in 1525 on the eve of the Spanish conquest.

Leon, Calixto. Husband of Catalina and father of Julia (Mrs Florencio Colque) and Isabel (Mrs Angel Colque).

Leon, Catalina. Wife of Calixto and mother of Julia (Mrs Florencio Colque) and Isabel (Mrs Angel Colque).

Lopez, Alberto. Brother of Cirilo Lopez and evangelical pastor.

Lopez, Antonio. Elder son of Cirilo and Francisca Lopez.

Lopez, Cirilo. Quechua-speaking evangelist from Sucre. Founded the Association of Evangelical Congregations in Oruro with Alberto Conde.

Lopez, Elias. Youngest son of Cirilo and Francisca Lopez.

Lopez, Francisca. Wife of Cirilo Lopez.

Montalvo, Valerio. Member of the Oruro church. Challenged Florencio Colque's leadership of the Association of Evangelical Congregations.

Morales, Alejandro. Owner of the *hacienda* in Lequepalca where Florencio Colque was born.

Morales, Eliseo. Owner of the *hacienda* in Lequepalca where Florencio Colque was born.

Pachacutec, Inca, 1391–1471. Acknowledged greatest ruler of the Inca empire. Pondered true identity of Viracocha.

Pérez, Emilio. Member of the Oruro congregation who fought for removal of the brothels on Cañada Strongest Street.

Pizarro, Francisco, 1475–1541. Spanish soldier-of-fortune who led the conquest of the Inca empire.

Poma, Tito. Resident of Lequepalca who first opposed, and later embraced, the gospel.

Quispe, Dionisio. Practising *curandero* from Lequepalca.

Quispe, Mario. Educator and pastor from La Paz. Father of Victor Quispe.

Quispe, Victor. Educator and pastor from La Paz. Son of Mario Quispe.

Ramos, Julian. Brother of Mrs Florencia Ramos Condori of Calapata.

Titicala, Ramón. Member of the Oruro church. Challenged Florencio Colque's leadership of the Association of Evangelical Congregations.

Vallejos, Antolín. Resident of Lequepalca who first opposed, and later embraced, the gospel.

Vedia Daza, Saul. Oruro district attorney who ordered removal of the brothels on Cañada Strongest Street.

Place Names

Altiplano (see map)

Amotar (somewhere near Calistía)

Antofagasta (on the coast of Chile)

Calapata (near Oruro, see map)

Calistía (near Lequepalca, see map)

Caracollo (near Oruro, see map)

Caranavi (in the Yungas, see map)

Chaco, the (see map)

Challapampa (near Oruro, see map)

Chicuela Alta (near Lequepalca, see map)

Coani (near Lequepalca, see map)

Cochabamba (see map)

Coipasa (salt flats)

Collpa (near Lequepalca, see map)

Colquiri (near Lequepalca, see map)

Cuti Bancarani (in the Yungas, see map)

Cuzco (in Peru)

Kami (near Cochabamba, see map)

La Paz (see map)

Lake Poopo (on the Altiplano, see map)

Lequepalca (see map)

Mount Illampu (near Lake Titicaca, see map)

Orán (in Argentina)

Oruro (see map)

Panama (in Central America)

Paria (near Oruro, see map)

Pasto Grande (near Oruro, see map)

Potosí peak (see map)

San Jose (near Oruro, see map)

Sorocachi (near Oruro, see map)

Sucre (see map)

Tarija (in the Chaco, see map)

Tiahuanacu (see map)

Tiraque (near Cochabamba, see map)

Toledo (near Oruro, see map)

Tupiza (near Villazón, see map)

Ucureña (near Cochabamba, see map)

Uyuni (near Oruro, see map)

Villazón (see map)

Yauricoya (near Oruro, see map)

Yocalla (near Lequepalca, see map)

Yungas, the (see map)

The First Song

A century before Columbus landed in the Americas, the Inca prince Cusi dreamed of Viracocha. Cusi had left Cuzco with a contingent of the royal army to patrol the southern reaches of the empire. One night as the prince slept, a tall man with flowing robes and bushy beard appeared to him.

'I am Viracocha,' he said to Cusi, 'child of the sun and brother to the Inca. I have come to warn you to return to Cuzco immediately. The Chankakuna have risen up against the emperor and laid siege to the city.'

Cusi obeyed the vision, returning at once with his soldiers to Cuzco where, as Viracocha had warned, the Chankakuna were making war on the capital. The prince's unexpected return took the aggressors by surprise. Cusi defeated the Chankakuna army, killing their king, Asto Huaraca, in hand-to-hand combat and saved the city. The grateful residents promptly elevated the intrepid prince to the throne. Upon his ascension, Cusi changed his name to Inca Pachacutec.

Inca Pachacutec would become the greatest ruler in the history of the empire. He possessed a fine intellect and boundless energy and gave the people wise laws. He built irrigation systems, roadways and fortresses, all of them engineering wonders. He also built temples. Pachacutec acknowledged that he owed his fortune to Viracocha and the young ruler expressed his gratitude by building a temple for the deity. It sat 50 miles south of Cuzco, on the spot where Viracocha appeared to Pachacutec in his dream.

When it came to religion, Inca Pachacutec displayed the same passion for excellence he brought to other matters of state. From childhood, he had heard the legends of Viracocha's dealings with his Inca forebears. The bearded figure clad in long robes fascinated him. The more he contemplated his vision of Viracocha and what it meant, the more intrigued he became with the deity. Pachacutec finally convened a council of priests in Koricancha, the majestic court of the Temple of the Sun in Cuzco. The Inca assigned the clergymen a daunting task: to establish the identity of Viracocha so that the Inca could worship him in the proper way.

The theologians waged a long and vigorous debate. When it ended, they had reached a startling conclusion. The mysterious Viracocha was none other than the Creator of the world. Their decision was based on the conclusion that Cusi had misunderstood Viracocha's relationship to Inti, the sun god. Viracocha was not Inti's son, the priests determined, but his *father*. This meant he was *Illa Tijsi*, the Origin of all being. Further proof of this was the fact that Viracocha had exercised omniscience by warning Cusi of the Chankakuna rebellion. Helping the prince defeat the enemy showed that Viracocha was omnipotent, as well. Only *Pachakamaj*, the Supreme Governor of the universe, possessed these attributes. Based upon their discussions in council, the priests announced a new name for the Creator of the world. Henceforth he was officially known as *Tijsi Viracocha Pachakamaj*. The title expressed, as accurately as possible, the full character of his divinity. In general usage, however, the Incas dropped the technical terms and called him simply 'Viracocha'.

Inca theologians revised their creation epic so that it harmonized with their belief about Viracocha. They affirmed that Viracocha created the first human beings, forming some of mud and sculpting others from rock, and left them buried underground. In the fullness of time, the people sprouted to the surface through openings in the earth such as springs, lakes, caves and mountain peaks. Tribes therefore could trace their ancestry to familiar landmarks. The Chayanta, for instance, considered themselves descendants of Potosí peak. The Killakas claimed to have originated in Lake Poopo. The Umasuyu believed themselves children of Mount Illampu. And so it went.

Satisfied that he had discovered the true identity of God, Pachacutec elevated Viracocha to the principal station in the Inca pantheon. A temple was built in the centre of Cuzco to house a new image of Viracocha encrusted with gold. In spite of his official patronage, however, Viracocha never captured the imagination of the masses. History shows that only the Inca nobility were careful to pay homage to the Creator of the world. The general population continued to worship Inti, the sun god. Imperial soldiers, in particular, trusted in Inti to give them victory in war and carried the sun god's standard before them into battle. Thus, as the empire expanded its conquest of the Andes, the sun god's notoriety spread among conquered peoples.

Nevertheless, Viracocha was not forgotten. Inca poets composed hymns in praise of the Creator. Some of the finest of these songs are attributed to the reign of Inca Pachacutec, the man who sought to unravel the mystery of Viracocha. The text of some hymns survived in oral form into the colonial era and were written down by the Spanish chronicler Cristobal de Molina. One of these is the 'First Prayer to the Creator,' which de Molina says was sung each year at the great festival of *Situwa Raymi*. There is no way of knowing if Pachacutec himself is the author, but it is reasonably certain the emperor knew the hymn and joined in singing it.

'First Prayer to the Creator'

Tijsi Viracocha	Root of being, Creator
Qaylla Viracocha	God, forever near.
T'ukapu ajnupuyuj	Lord of long vestments,
Viracocha	The Dazzling One.
Kamaj, churaj	One who governs and provides,
Ñispa ruraj	Who created by simply speaking.
Qhari Kachun	'Become man.'
Warmi Kachun	'Become woman.'

1

Orphan, 1940

Little Florencio sensed that something was terribly wrong with his father. Gregorio Colque had not risen from his bed for some days and the fever was worsening. The adults knew this and moved cautiously about the tiny adobe house, speaking in whispers, as though careless noise might arouse the fury of Gregorio's sickness. From the doorway Florencio stared at his father lying on the piled sheepskins. Señor Colque had not spoken for nearly 24 hours. When his eyelids opened, the sightless pupils rolled backward in the sockets. Florencio did not know his father was in a coma. He was too young to understand such things. Nor did he know what this thing was that the adults called 'a plague'.

Florencio did understand that his father was helpless and this hurt him. Gregorio was a strong and capable man, popular in Lequepalca for his cheerful disposition and hard-working ways. The Colques were a respected family in their community. Their surname was taken from the word for 'silver' in Aymara and Quechua, the languages of the ancient empires. It indicated that Colques were an important clan and the community treated them with a certain deference.

Gregorio lived up to his family's stature and earned the respect of his neighbours. He was not a drunkard, although on holidays and special occasions he drank himself into a stupor on *chicha*, a potent, home-brewed corn beer. *Chicha* was a common vice among Andean peoples, however, so no one begrudged Gregorio his drinking binges, so long as he did not hurt anyone.

There was the time when Florencio was an infant that his parents' drinking nearly caused him serious injury. It happened at Carnival, the three-day festival just before the onset of Lent, when the town flung itself into unbridled celebration. Dancers dressed in elaborate costumes and pranced in the streets in honour of the devil. The children delighted themselves with water fights. *Chicha* flowed freely and most of the revellers remained intoxicated for days.

One afternoon during a downpour of rain, a drunken Gregorio delighted himself by stomping about in a mud puddle. When his wife, Valentina, asked him what he was doing, he said he intended to splash all the water out of the puddle. The idea struck her fancy so she began to help, tromping the muddy water in time to the carnival music. Like all peasant women, Valentina carried her infant son on her back. She had tightly wrapped Florencio in woollen bandages and tied him up in her *aguayo*, the brightly coloured blanket that served as backpack and cradle. As Valentina danced, her *aguayo* hindered her movements. In her foggy stupor, she forgot what the bundle contained and carelessly cast it off her shoulders. The *aguayo*, with little Florencio inside, thudded to the ground. Luckily the child landed in soft mud and suffered no broken bones.

Accidents aside, the Colques were good parents to their son and his older sister Máxima. It was true that Gregorio and Valentina sometimes fought, and if Gregorio were drunk, their fights sometimes came to blows. But once, after little Florencio protested a heated argument between his parents with terrified bawling, the battles diminished. In fact, of all the homes in Lequepalca, the Colques' was one of the happiest.

An epidemic, however, is no respecter of persons. Once the plague had closed its deadly grip on Gregorio Colque, the young husband and father was doomed. With his loved ones looking on helplessly, Gregorio drew a last gasping breath and then lay still. Others followed him into eternity as the plague advanced. Florencio lost both his paternal grandparents and a cousin. Nor were the Colques the only household in Lequepalca touched by tragedy. The plague swept through the village and on to neighbouring mountain communities. As it moved relentlessly through the tiny clusters of thatched adobe houses, the fever killed one or two persons in each. Rarely did it wipe out an entire family, however. In one home, a young couple died leaving three small children. In another family of seven, only a teenage boy succumbed.

As the plague reaped its grim harvest, a shortage of gravediggers developed. Farmers were called in from the fields to perform the sombre task of collecting and burying corpses. Only a few volunteered for the dangerous task of interring the dead and they were unable to keep pace with the advance of the fever. Hours passed after Gregorio's death before two men appeared at the door to bear away his remains. Florencio watched mutely as they wrapped his father's body in his heavy, woollen blanket, laid the rigid bundle on a ladder and secured it with ropes. On signal, the men heaved the litter onto their shoulders and started off toward the cemetery at a brisk trot. Public officials did not permit families to accompany their loved ones to the burial for fear of spreading the epidemic. The Colques could only stand at the door of their humble home and watch the men bear Gregorio away to his grave.

Two weeks after Gregorio Colque's death the plague subsided in Lequepalca. Farmers returned to their fields and life once more took on its familiar rhythm. Florencio had not wept for his father, being too young to comprehend the tragedy. Nor was he encouraged to mourn. His aunts and uncles wept uncontrollably, however, when they came to console Valentina. They patted Florencio on the head and sobbed, 'Don't you cry, little man. Everything is going to be all right.' Florencio mistook their puzzling behaviour for some kind of adult joke, and giggled at the mourners. Months would pass before the toddler would grasp the meaning of his father's death. On the first day of November, Florencio watched his mother bake bread to place on his father's tomb. Valentina was following an All Saints' Day custom strictly observed in Bolivia. She explained to her little son that she would take the bread to the cemetery so that Gregorio could enjoy his favourite treat in the land of the dead. Suddenly, it occurred to Florencio that this meant his father was truly gone, which meant that he would never see him again. Florencio began to cry.

Florencio's mother wept as well. But in a remarkably short time, Valentina put her grief for Gregorio behind her. She had to. Like other young widows in peasant villages throughout the mountains, Valentina faced an urgent challenge: keeping herself and her two small children alive.

* * *

One hour before dawn, Valentina Vallejos Colque awoke and rubbed the sleep from her eyes. She would have preferred to remain in bed until the sun rose and warmed the chill mountain air, but that was a luxury she could not afford. Now that Valentina was her family's sole breadwinner, she had to begin her workday early. She threw off the woollen blankets and rose from the cosy pile of sheepskins.

Valentina checked her sleeping children, then picked up her milk pails and stepped outside. In the feeble light, she made her way to the sheepfold to begin milking. Valentina had to start this chore early because the lambs had been separated from their mothers all night and could not suckle until the ewes were milked. She would make cheese of the milk. Six pints of sheep milk produced one pound of cheese. It took two or three ewes to render one pint of milk. Valentina had a lot of sheep to milk this morning.

The sun was well up by the time Valentina finished and returned the hungry lambs to their mothers. She carried the foaming pails back to the house where Florencio and Máxima were still sleeping soundly. 'Time to get up, children!' Valentina called, shaking them awake. Once the little ones were on their feet, their mother dispatched them on their morning chores. Florencio went to cut *th'ola* shrubs for the cooking fire and Máxima fetched water from the river.

The little girl did not have a long walk. The adobe house in which three generations of Colques had lived sat on a low bluff just above the river. Her grandfather built it there in order to be near water. The hut had one door, no windows, a dirt floor and no paint anywhere. But it kept out the cold, the wind and the rain, which is all that any house, however grand or humble, is required to do. Valentina stirred the fire in the corner pit and added a few *th'ola* branches. The flames were soon licking the blackened bottom of the kettle in which she cooked all her family's meals. Today, as on most mornings, Valentina prepared *quinua* porridge. 'Come, eat the *lawa*,' Valentina called to her children when the thick soup was ready. Florencio and Máxima joined their mother on the dirt floor around the cooking fire.

Had they been other children, they might have complained. 'What? *lawa* for breakfast again!' Andean peasants considered *quinua* porridge a poor meal, quite inferior to the white bread and sweet tea that affluent city dwellers ate for breakfast. But since Gregorio's death, Valentina could not afford such treats. Actually, Florencio and Máxima were fortunate to have *quinua* in place of rice and white bread. A tiny seed resembling sesame, *quinua* is packed with amino acids. The first humans to settle the Andes discovered the grain growing wild there because only in extreme altitudes can it receive the intense sunlight it needs to mature. More nutritious than soya beans, *quinua* ranks among nature's perfect foods. Eating *quinua* for breakfast instead of white bread kept peasant children like Florencio and Máxima from dying of malnutrition.

Once the children finished eating, Valentina sent them out to pasture the family's small herd of livestock. Florencio and Máxima drove the sheep and llamas out of the stone corral and up the steep mountain slope. The little boy carried a sling to launch rocks at the animals when they strayed into fields of potatoes or barley. Máxima followed the flock, deftly twirling a hand spindle. The simple tool turned sheep wool into sturdy thread. Like every female of her race, Máxima worked with her spindle whenever her hands were free, while resting in the house, while pasturing sheep, while walking along mountain paths.

It was an endless project. Andean women had to produce thousands of yards of woollen thread each year for family clothing.

When she had spun enough thread to make cloth for a pair of pants or a waistcoat, Señora Colque would take it to her brother-in-law for weaving. Weaving was largely a male craft in Lequepalca, passed down from father to son for generations. Florencio's uncle worked steadily for one week to manufacture enough cloth for a new suit of clothes. He sat at the wooden loom from daylight to dusk, sliding the shuttle back and forth through the warp and jamming the woof together with a hand batten. Valentina paid him for his work with *quinua* and potatoes. During colonial times, homespun Andean woollens fetched high prices in Europe, nearly equalling in value the enormous quantities of the gold and silver imported from South America. It was said that some Spanish merchants chained native labourers to their looms to force them to work the long hours necessary to meet the demand for woollen cloth.

As the Colque children made their way up the mountainside with the sheep and llamas, their mother stayed home making cheese. Valentina heated sheep milk in the iron kettle and skimmed off the whey. She added rennet, a pinch of paste scraped from the dried stomach of a suckling lamb, to the curds, kneaded the warm mass with her hands and pressed it into straw moulds. The end product was similar in texture to cottage cheese but pungent. It needed only a day or two to age before going to market. When she finished her cheese-making, Valentina shouldered her hoe and set off for the potato field. Normally, women did not work in the fields. But since Gregorio's death, Valentina had to do her husband's work as well as her own. She made her way briskly along the trail, worried that she would be late to work. During planting season the crew started early.

The potato crop was a first priority for villagers in Lequepalca. Potatoes were the staple of their diet and had been the staff of life in the mountains for millennia. Tradition says that the potato was a gift of the gods. When sowing potatoes, Lequepalca farmers offered sacrifices to Pachamama, Mother of the Earth, to express their gratitude for her bounty and their hopes for a substantial crop. The importance of the potato to Quechua people has even left its mark on their native tongue. Most languages have only one word to identify the lowly vegetable, but Quechua uses at least two hundred terms to differentiate a multitude of potato varieties – *emilia, waycu, koli, waycha, runa, arichuo, luki, ajawiri, lisa, pitocwayaka* – and many more.

Like all Andean cooks, Valentina knew which variety of potato to bake in the fire pit, which tasted best fried and which went into soups. During the trying times after Gregorio's death, Valentina had precious little else to put in her soups besides potatoes, *quinua* and *chuño*. *Chuño* was the first food man learned to preserve with freeze-drying. In the middle of winter when nights are coldest, Andean peasants spread potatoes out on the open ground. For three successive nights, the potatoes freeze rock-solid. On three successive mornings, they thaw to mush. On the final morning, farmers gather the soggy potatoes into piles, remove their sandals and stomp barefoot on them to squeeze out any remaining moisture. The process transforms potatoes into dry, feather-light *chuño*. Farmers can store *chuño* for years without spoilage.

The sun was well above the mountain peaks when Valentina finally reached the potato field. Today she was working for the *patrón* in order to pay rent on the small parcel of land where she lived. The foreman saw Valentina straggling in and met her with a hard look.

'What's this? Late again?'

'Yes, you must excuse me, but I was making cheese this morning,' Valentina explained. While she spoke to the foreman, she carefully kept her gaze on the ground at her feet.

'How many cheeses did you make?' the foreman asked, peering intently into Valentina's downcast face.

Just two, Valentina lied. She did not want the foreman to know about all her cheeses. She would have to deliver most of them to the *patrón* anyway to help pay the rent on her land. But she was hoping to sell some on the side to earn a little extra cash.

'Bring me one of them tomorrow,' he said. 'I must test the quality.'

Valentina would obey. She had no choice if she hoped to remain in the good graces of the foreman. He had already let it be known that Valentina was not pulling her fair share of the work. She could not handle a yoke of oxen, so she could not do any ploughing. She could dig potato rows, and applied herself to the backbreaking labour without complaint. Yet even in this, she could not keep pace with the men. She hoped the foreman would not mention this to the *patrón*, who perhaps might feel justified in allotting her extra work to pay the rent.

These thoughts occupied Valentina as she worked through the morning. But at noon, when she sat down to eat lunch, her thoughts turned to her two young children. Where would they be at this hour? What adventures had they encountered during their wanderings with the sheep and llamas? She munched on toasted corn and sipped a beverage of barley and wondered where Florencio and Máxima might be eating lunch.

The sun would set that evening before Valentina could talk about the day with her children. Arriving home in the twilight, she helped Florencio and Máxima corral the sheep, separating the lambs from their mothers as usual. Then she sent Máxima to fetch water from the river and Florencio to gather *th'ola* shrubs for the cooking fire. After their supper of *quinua* porridge and boiled potatoes, the children went to bed. As usual, Valentina stayed up a while longer, spinning woollen thread by the dim light of her kerosene lamp. Sometime around 9 p.m. – although she had no clock to tell the hour – she lay down on her sheepskin mattress. Without undressing, she pulled the heavy blankets over herself and fell into an exhausted sleep.

Valentina Vallejos Colque and her two young children, like everyone in Lequepalca, lived off the land. The land was the most valuable commodity in their Andean universe. It is said that the ancient Incas placed no commercial value on gold and silver. They used the precious metals only to decorate temples, never for coins or currency. The value of land, on the other hand, could not be calculated. After all, the precious land gave them the gold and silver, as well as everything else in their universe. The earth upon which Valentina and her two children spent each day provided their every need. It gave them food and clothing. It provided them with mud and straw to build their home and clay to fashion their household pottery. The land gave them herbs to cure their illnesses and received the bodies of loved ones whose illnesses proved incurable. Valentina knew all she needed to know about the land in order to survive in her tiny house in Lequepalca and raise her small children. She had only to work 16 hours a day, 7 days a week at the grinding task of survival. This she was prepared to do.

*   *   *

Valentina might have succeeded in raising her two children to adulthood in Lequepalca, except for one thing: she had to rent her land. The 20 acres on which the Colque home sat, like the rest of the land in Lequepalca, belonged to Alejandro and Eliseo Morales. Their *hacienda* included all the land between Coani and Yocalla, in fact, some 75 square miles of real estate. The labour required to cultivate such a tract of land was substantial, but the owners did little of it themselves. Two hundred peasant families living on the *hacienda* worked for the Morales family in exchange for the right to live on the land.

Haciendas were a legacy of the Spanish conquest. In 1534, soon after he had vanquished Inca Atahualpa, Francisco Pizarro marched into Cuzco and declared the city and its provinces subject to the Spanish crown. The area in question included the future nations of Peru, Ecuador and Bolivia, as well as parts of Argentina and Chile. Upon Pizarro's declaration, these conquered lands henceforth belonged to the King of Spain and would be known as a 'viceroyalty'.

Spain intended to incorporate the Inca empire into its realm without disrupting, as much as practicable, the existing social order. Thus, after eliminating the Inca and dismantling the empire, Pizarro was instructed to respect the rule of the *kurakas*, native provincial governors. *Kurakas* who pledged allegiance to Charles V were allowed to continue governing their provinces.

Except for annual tax levies, these local rulers experienced little interference in their affairs.

Inevitably, some *kurakas* rebelled against the Spanish and were eliminated. In their place, the viceroys appointed *encomenderos* to supervise native communities. Typically an officer of the Spanish army, the *encomendero* did not own the land he managed. Legal title remained firmly in the hands of the crown. However, the *encomendero* was entitled to a yearly tribute from the natives living under his governance. Every year they contributed livestock, potatoes, grain, woollen cloth, hides and spices, a portion of all the goods they raised or manufactured. The *encomendero* was allowed to keep part of the tribute as personal income. The remainder was to be invested in a church to provide for the religious instruction of the natives.

During the early colonial period, *encomenderos* ruled a relatively small percentage of the rural villages in the Andes. Free communities, governed by native *kurakas*, far outnumbered the *encomiendas*. But then two things happened that shifted the balance of power in favour of the Europeans. The first was a tragedy that historians refer to as 'The Great Dying'. Native Americans, living in isolation from the Old World for thousands of years, did not develop natural immunity to diseases such as smallpox and measles. This meant that, from the moment white men first set foot on American soil, millions of red men were condemned to death by plague. Mosquitoes carried malaria from Panama to South America, and the disease began killing people in the Andes even before Pizarro landed on the coast of Peru. Once the Spanish began arriving *en masse*, epidemics swept the region. The Great Dying nearly emptied parts of the conquered empire. The population of the territory encompassing southern Peru, for example, plunged from five million during the Inca era to 300,000 by the end of the seventeenth century.

Another element that forever altered the social structure in the Andes was silver. In 1545, a Spanish soldier discovered the world's largest known deposit of silver at Potosí. The Spanish were eager to exploit the riches and sent tens of thousands of native Americans to work the mines, furthering emptying rural villages. Francisco Toledo, the Spanish viceroy who presided over the silver rush, faced a huge administrative challenge: how to coerce the dwindling populations in rural villages to produce enough surplus food to feed the burgeoning population of miners in Potosí who, in turn, produced the silver that was making Spain wealthy.

Toledo's solution was to encourage the growth of *haciendas*. Like the traditional *encomiendas*, *haciendas* were run by Spaniards. Unlike an *encomienda*, a *hacienda* was privately owned. The *hacienda* produced a surplus of food and goods. But unlike the *encomienda*, this surplus did not go to build churches. It was sold to mining companies in Potosí at a handsome profit.

The *hacienda* owner was called a *patrón*. He was typically a Spaniard who paid taxes on his property to the crown. Workers on the hacienda were *colonos*, native Americans who paid rent to the *patrón* for the right to live on his property. Rent was generally collected in labour. The *patrón*, of course, determined the amount of work necessary to pay the rent. When the *patrón* ordered his *colonos* to work, they worked. When he ordered them to stop working, they stopped.

The great silver rush lasted nearly 150 years. It ended only when ground water began seeping into the hundreds of mining shafts dug into Potosí peak, flooding out the miners. By that time, *haciendas* had effectively taken hold in the Andes, controlling one-third of all cultivated land. When the profits from silver declined, however, so did the profitability of the *haciendas*. Some *patrones* cut back production, others abandoned their estates to live in the cities cropping up along the Pacific coast and in low-lying valleys. Hardly any sold their properties, however. *Haciendas* would exist in the Andes for a long time yet.

The 1880s witnessed a revival in the mining industry, spurred by the invention of steam engines that pumped ground water out of the mine shafts. Miners returned to Potosí in droves. Agribusiness *a la hacienda* revived. In Bolivia, which was now an independent republic, the rush for farm land was as fierce as the rush for silver.

Most of the countryside still belonged to native free communities, so white men had to take legal measures to expropriate the land. Bolivia had recently lost a costly war with Chile and the government was desperate to replenish the national budget. In order to raise revenue, politicians in La Paz declared all communal-owned property public lands. Native free communities were communal-owned properties, of course, the only such lands in the republic. If a buyer could come up with the purchase price of a piece of this 'public' land, the government sold it to him. The local residents, who had worked the land for centuries, were not party to the transaction. Often, they knew nothing of the transfer until the new owner showed up to survey his acquisition and set the boundaries. The whole business gave rise to a curious nickname for the new landlords. They were called 'stake-outers'. To the natives, it appeared that, in order to acquire the land they wanted, these *patrones* simply had to drive stakes around the perimeter of the property and it was theirs.

Of course, there had been a transfer of money. The government received the money, the stake-outer got the land and the natives got nothing. They had no recourse but to offer themselves as *colonos* to the new *patrón*.

* * *

Like all *colonos* in Lequepalca, Gregorio Colque laboured in the *patrón*'s fields in exchange for the privilege of living on the *hacienda* and farming his small plot of land. He had not resented the arrangement. Conditions on the Morales estate were more tolerable than many. The Morales family cultivated only about 650 acres of their property. This required the *colonos* to work only two weeks during planting season, two weeks while the crop was in the ground to keep the weeds down and one month at harvest time.

But when Gregorio Colque died, his widow Valentina found it impossible to fulfil her obligations to the *patrón* and take care of her two small children at the same time. By custom, a widow was considered part of her husband's family. This allowed her to continue to live in her husband's house. Her in-laws were expected to provide for her and her children. But Valentina was unable to take advantage of this custom because Gregorio's parents had also died in the plague. The only living relative upon whom she could depend was Gregorio's older brother, Casmiro. Casmiro would have helped his sister-in-law, as custom dictated, had it not been for an unfortunate set of circumstances that obliged Casmiro to leave Lequepalca in haste.

Casmiro had good reason for leaving. In addition to the regular work of cultivating the *patrón*'s crops, *colonos* took turns pasturing the Moraleses' sheep and llamas. The herd numbered nearly 1,000 animals so the job was full-time. The assignment lasted for one year. A man was required to do it but once during his lifetime. Since he could not raise any crops for himself and his family the year he served as *hacienda* shepherd, a *colono* was careful to set aside extra stores of food against the day when the job would fall to him.

Gregorio Colque had just begun his term as *hacienda* shepherd when he took sick and died. The *patrón* decided his brother Casmiro should replace him. 'You are going to be my shepherd this year in place of Gregorio,' Señor Morales told him one day.

Casmiro was unwilling to accept the chore because he had already served his year-long term. As well, he was unprepared to accept it because he did not have enough reserves of potatoes and *chuño* to feed his wife and children for an entire year. So he did the sort of thing a man in a desperate situation will do. Without telling anyone, he gathered up his animals and loaded them with food and tools. His wife gathered up the children and loaded them with her household goods. By the light of the moon, Casmiro pulled down his house and barn. When the sun rose the following morning, he and his family had disappeared from Lequepalca.

Casmiro resettled in a village across the border in the La Paz department. Casmiro chose this refuge because it was a free community not under the jurisdiction of a *patrón*. He feared no reprisal for abandoning Señor Morales. Casmiro hired himself out to local farmers, who paid him as best they could. In solving his problem with the *patrón*, Casmiro created another one for Valentina. With none of her in-laws remaining on the Colque homestead, Valentina had no choice but to leave the house she had shared with her dead husband. She moved in with her sister, Justina.

Justina was married to Máximo Colque. Although he had the same surname as Gregorio, Máximo was of a different clan. He was under no obligation to help Valentina and the arrangement soon proved awkward. One day Máximo made a diplomatic suggestion.

'I have been talking with some folks from Challapampa,' he said. 'They told me that they have plenty of wool there and are looking for women to knit. I think it would be good if you tried that for a while, Valentina.'

Valentina, Máxima and Florencio moved from Lequepalca to a tiny house in Challapampa. Valentina knitted nine hours a day in order to feed her family. Florencio worked as well, carding wool. Máxima helped with spinning the yarn.

Valentina decided to try her hand at cutting firewood to supplement her meagre income. When she found neighbours willing to loan her a pair of burros, she began making trips to Oruro to sell firewood in the city market.

On one of these trips to Oruro, friends told Valentina of work at the brick yards. The yards were looking for women to mould ceramic roofing tiles, they said. It sounded to Valentina as if she could make more money in the brick yards than with knitting. She told her friends, however, that she would have to think it over. She was not sure she should uproot her children and bring them to live in a city like Oruro.

Later that afternoon, Valentina, Máxima and Florencio set out for home with the borrowed burros. The animals were now loaded with bread, sugar and rice Valentina had bought with earnings from the firewood. The Colques would have to make part of the journey in the dark, but they knew the path well and did not worry about losing their way. While they were some distance from home, however, a thunderstorm hit. The stars disappeared, as well as all familiar landmarks, and Valentina worried that Máxima and Florencio would get lost. Thus distracted, she did not notice that one of the burros went missing from her little caravan. Only upon arriving at her door did she discover, to her horror, that the animal was not with them.

Valentina was really worried now. How would she repay her neighbours for the lost burro? Despite her exhaustion, Valentina did not sleep that night. At first light, she retraced her steps towards Oruro. She covered nearly three miles before she found the burro, grazing peacefully by the side of the trail. Amazingly, his load of groceries was still intact. Valentina had not seen such a lovely burro in all her life.

She had been fortunate, indeed. But the trauma prompted Valentina to think seriously about other means of survival. She decided to apply for work at the Oruro brickyards after all.

2

Miners and Merchants

'So, you want a job, eh?' The brickyard owner looked closely at Valentina Vallejos Colque and her two children. The mother appeared strong and healthy. With a bit of supervision she could turn into a decent hand. Her boy looked about seven or eight, too young to do much heavy work, probably. He seemed an alert little fellow. A bit shy, but polite to his elders. The girl, Máxima, would not be much help, he decided. Even though she was at least ten, she was thin and frail.

After sizing up the family, the brickmaker said, 'Okay, this is the deal. You start work at 9 a.m., work until 7 p.m. Sundays off. I pay you for every thousand units you produce. In addition, I give you a free room and you can buy groceries at our company store.' Valentina considered this for a moment. 'How about Saturdays?' she said. 'I have to have some time for marketing.'

'Okay, you can have Saturday afternoons off, as long as you came back here to sleep.' Since the man was paying her by piece work it did not matter to him that she took extra time off, but he did want somebody around at night to keep an eye on the place.

Valentine asked to see the living quarters. The brickmaker led them to a tiny cubicle at the back of the yard. It had no windows, an uneven dirt floor and a leaky roof. But Valentina was satisfied that she could make it liveable with the sheepskins and kerosene lamps she had brought from Lequepalca. She could kindle her cooking fires outside. Straw and sheep dung would have to do for fuel, since no *th'ola* shrubs grew on the barren flats surrounding the brickyard.

'When do I start?' she asked the foreman.

'Tomorrow morning. You can sleep here tonight.'

'One thing more,' Valentine said, gazing at the ground at her feet. 'I have no money. Will you give me the first week's groceries on credit?' A pause, then she looked up sharply. 'I can't work if I can't eat.'

The man was not particularly surprised by the request. Most of the people he hired were destitute, otherwise they would not be looking for work in a brickyard. 'All right,' he said. As an afterthought, he added, 'How about the boy? He looks like he could be of some help. At least until you can get out of debt.'

Valentina stood silently for a moment as she thought about this. Florencio was very young. Most boys his age were still herding sheep or, if their parents had the means, starting school. But then, most boys his age had fathers. Valentina looked at Florencio, then at the foreman and quickly nodded her head.

The following morning, Florencio and his mother made their first batch of bricks under the watchful eye of the brickyard owner. They mixed ten wheelbarrows of clay with water, added three wheelbarrows of ashes and two of sheep dung. Florencio and his mother kneaded the mixture with bare feet until well blended. They packed the wet clay into brick moulds and deposited the moulded bricks onto drying boards in the oven. After trimming the soft bricks of lumps, they repeated the procedure until bricks filled the oven. The owner took over from there, firing the brick and grading the finished product.

One batch of the clay-ash-dung mixture rendered approximately 470 bricks. For every thousand bricks the Colques produced, the owner paid them one peso. Months passed before they saw any cash money, however. Each week they earned just enough to pay their bill at the company store. When the day came that Valentina, with Florencio's help, finally paid the last of her debt to the store, she told the brickyard owner she was quitting.

'Why?' he asked, unhappy to lose a good hand.

'A friend has offered me the chance to open a shop in the

central market,' she replied. 'I think I can make a go of it. At least, I am going to try.'

Valentina's confident tone convinced the brickmaker that it was futile to argue. Her mind was made up.

'What about the boy?' he asked. Florencio had proven himself a fair worker at the brickyard. The owner did not want to lose him, as well. 'Tell you what,' the man said, 'if Florencio keeps working for me, you can keep your room here.'

Valentina waited a moment before replying. She had anticipated the offer, seeing that the brickmaker had regard for her son's ability. However, she did not want to appear too eager to accept. The owner must not think he was doing her a favour.

'Will you pay him cash wages?' she asked.

'Of course.' The man had already calculated that Florencio was worth his wages.

Valentina gave a quick nod. Florencio would keep making bricks.

For the next two years, the boy made bricks. As a novice, Florencio could turn out only 150 bricks a day. His six-day working week earned him one peso. Over time, however, he increased his daily production to 300 bricks, in effect doubling his wages. The boy worked hard for the money. The lye in the mortar dried out his hands. He rubbed motor oil on them every day, but still the skin cracked and bled. On winter mornings he had to break the ice on the pond that supplied the yard in order to get the water for his batches. His feet went numb from stomping the freezing mixture. To keep them warm, he ferried the brick moulds back and forth to the oven at a brisk trot.

The hard work that Florencio did on weekdays conditioned him for the important pastime he enjoyed at weekends: football. Never a Sunday passed that the boy did not join in some game on a back street or open space. He was good at football. Florencio was short for his age, but sturdy and quick. In games with peers he was always one of the first chosen for the side. He could usually give a good account of himself, as well, when he played older boys.

After several months' diligence at the brickyard, Florencio managed to save three pesos from his wages. 'I'm going to use the money to buy a pair of shoes,' he told his mother.

His announcement puzzled Valentina. Her children had never asked for a pair of shoes in their lives. Like other peasant children, they wore sandals cut from llama hide or old car tyres. 'What do you want shoes for?' she asked.

'For Sundays,' he replied.

This puzzled Valentina even more. Florencio had never been vain about his appearance. She could not imagine him wanting a pair of Sunday shoes to show off to his friends. But then, the boy worked hard at the brickyard. He deserved a reward. If Florencio wanted shoes, shoes he would have.

'Go ahead, then,' she said, smiling faintly. 'It's your money.'

Florencio disappeared in the direction of the central market. An hour later he returned, carrying a pair of brand-new shoes slung over his shoulder and grinning from ear to ear. Valentina chuckled as she examined his purchase. Of course Florencio would want these shoes for Sunday. They were football shoes!

* * *

Oruro, the city on the Altiplano.

The Altiplano of South America is one of the world's odd geographical phenomena. A vast expanse spanning Peru, Bolivia and Chile, it is as flat and featureless as the Great Plains of the United States. However, it is distinct from other flatlands on the planet in that its average elevation is 13,000 feet above sea level. For a geographical analogy, one might imagine the Siberian steppe raised to the height of the Swiss Alps.

The Altiplano is cold, colourless and dusty. It does offer the visitor one thing in abundance – space. Some parts are so flat and vegetation so sparse that automobiles make their own roads, wandering over the plain like random beetles. In the south, arable land gives way to immense salt flats at Uyuni and Coipasa. The flats cover an area nearly half the size of England, but their inhospitable environment supports almost no life forms, animal or vegetable.

Despite the immense empty spaces, Oruro, the principal population centre in the middle of the Altiplano, is a compact city. Lake Oruro, whose waters annually flood the town's southern outskirts, keeps urbanization from expanding in that direction. On the north and west, a series of peaks jut out of the plain, obstructing development. Instead of sprawling across the flat expanse like, say, Oklahoma City, Oruro is pinched and crowded. *Orureños*, however, do not begrudge the geographical hedges around their city. The lake gives them fish and the peaks supplied the treasure that put Oruro on the map: silver.

Silver ore was first discovered there in 1595. The resulting rush caused the population to swell to 20,000 souls by the year 1606, when the Spanish crown recognized Oruro as a municipality and granted it rights to levy taxes. By the mid-seventeenth century, Oruro claimed a population of 75,000, making it the second largest city in South America. Potosí, a mining town 200 miles to the southeast, was the largest. The silver vein Spanish soldiers discovered there soon after their conquest of the Incas transformed Potosí into an immense city. A census taken in 1648 revealed a population of 160,000, making Potosí by far the largest city in the Western Hemisphere. In fact, at that time, Potosí was the second largest metropolitan area in the world, after Paris.

The rest of the New World cities in that age were little more than hamlets compared to Potosí and Oruro. Lima had grown to only 25,000 residents by 1648, despite its prominence as the capital of the viceroyalty of Peru. Buenos Aires was an insignificant village, beset by pirates and Indians. Boston, the largest European settlement in North America, had fewer than 4,000 people. New York City did not yet exist.

Bolivian writers have said, with only mild exaggeration, that the Spanish extracted enough silver from mines in the Andes to build a bridge from Potosí to Madrid. It is a fact that when the fabulous riches played out, the exodus of fortune-seekers emptied both Potosí and Oruro. By 1750, fewer than 25,000 remained in Potosí. Oruro fared no better. A census taken in 1848 revealed that only 5,600 people remained of the multitudes that thronged its streets two centuries before.

The Antofagasta to Oruro railroad, completed by British engineers in 1892, sparked a new surge in the city's fortunes. With the advent of rail transport, Oruro became Bolivia's 'dry gateway' to the Pacific Ocean. Nearly every commodity imported from abroad and exported to foreign markets passed through the city on the Altiplano. Early in the twentieth century, tin replaced silver as Bolivia's chief export. Demand for the metal soared due to the rise of the commercial canning industry. During the two World Wars, demand reached such proportions that Oruro built its own foundry. From then on, the city processed most of Bolivia's tin and shipped it overseas. Mining companies established their head-quarters in Oruro and the international consortiums that bought its tin followed suit. These enterprises, in turn, attracted banks and brokerage houses. Merchants followed to market machinery, tools, clothing and groceries to the miners and European luxury goods to the businessmen.

As is the case in most boom towns, the population of the city was overwhelmingly male. The railroad and mining industries attracted thousands of single men. Unbalanced demographics gave rise to another business that expanded rapidly in the local economy: prostitution. Brothel operators discovered that lonely miners made good clients. They also learned that they could not find enough employees from among the local female population. The newly opened railroad provided the solution. Bordellos could bring women by train from Chile. Foreign prostitutes found the arrangement advantageous. They could ply their trade in anonymity and, after a few months' work, return home to invest their earnings in real estate or a small business. The Oruro brothels hired so many Chilean women that *chilena* soon became the local euphemism for 'harlot'.

At least one *chilena* came to town to stay. A woman known as Doña Consuelo bought 400 square metres of land in a working

class neighbourhood on the north edge of the city and opened a
brothel. Situated on Cañada Strongest Street, Doña Consuelo's
house became known for its cleanliness and discretion. Her
customers included leading businessmen, professionals, police
and city officials. Her distinguished clientele guaranteed that she
would be in business a long time.

This was Oruro, the city on the Altiplano. The hustling,
bustling, dry, dusty, crowded city that enticed Gregorio Colque's
widow, Valentina, from her home in Lequepalca. Perhaps it was
not the healthiest environment in which to rear her two young
children. But Oruro offered her little family something Lequepalca could not: a chance to survive.

* * *

After two years at the brickyards, Valentina found Florencio
another job. One of the regular customers at her tiny shop in the
market was the wife of a railway official. The woman asked
Valentina if her son would like work as a house boy. Though
the salary she offered was less than Florencio earned at brick-
making, the job included the irresistible fringe benefits of free
room and board at the railway official's home.

Florencio's new employer lived in a comfortable house in
the centre of town. Nearly every family in that neighbourhood
employed boys like Florencio to do household chores. Every day
he brought firewood from the market and water from the public
tap in the street. He also washed dishes, swept the sidewalk and
carried a hot lunch to his employer at the train station every
noon. His tasks were menial but they kept him busy most of his
waking hours. The rare occasions he was allowed time off, he
played football.

Only two features of the job were unpleasant. First, Florencio
rarely saw his mother or sister. Valentina lived alone in another
part of town. She had sent Máxima back to Lequepalca to live
with relatives. The young girl had grown thin and sickly living
in the city and her mother hoped the robust environment of the

country would bring back her health. Valentina was too tied to her shop in the market to visit either of her children much. In fact, Florencio saw her only twice during the six months he worked for the railway official.

That was the other unpleasant feature about Florencio's houseboy job, it lasted merely six months. The railway company transferred his boss to La Paz and Florencio was out of work. He soon found another job, once again through his mother. Some of Valentina's relatives had taken jobs in the San Jose tin mine, Oruro's largest. Valentina went to them and explained that Florencio needed to find work, urgently. Her cousins promised they would speak to the foreman. A few days later, Florencio reported to the San Jose for his first shift in the mine.

That day as he descended into the mineshaft, the boy experienced both fascination and fright. Fascination because the mine was so different from what he had imagined. It was a warm and quiet place. The sounds of hammer and chisel echoed only faintly through the subterranean corridors. No wonder, he thought, that miners believed the shafts to be enchanted. For them the underground was the domain of the devil. The miners obliquely referred to him as *El Tio*, 'the Uncle'. When Florencio descended into the mineshaft, he believed he was entering Satan's territory. That was why he was frightened. He was not the only one. Miners maintained a shrine to *El Tio* near the mineshaft entrance, and always upon entering, they were careful to leave a gift of coca leaves or cigarettes. The donations guaranteed protection from accident and brought luck in finding rich veins of ore. On the first Friday of every month, they sacrificed a rooster, a lamb or a white llama to ensure *El Tio*'s benevolence.

Florencio's awe of the underground soon diminished, however, due to the exhausting work assigned him. His job was to push the loaded ore trams to the dumping station and back again. The labour required no experience and minimum training. A strong back and plenty of stamina, however, were indispensable. To perform the task, Florencio followed the example of his adult workmates and took up chewing coca leaf.

Andean miners had formed the habit centuries before. The Incas were acquainted with 'the leaf' and considered it sacred. For that reason, Inca emperors restricted its use to holidays, weddings and other festive occasions. The Spanish viceroys were not so prudent. Under intense pressure from Spain to extract as much precious metal as possible from the Andes, they searched for means to increase the miners' productivity. Coca provided a cost-effective solution. A mild narcotic, coca masks fatigue and suppresses appetite. It also speeds up the body's cardiovascular tempo, furnishing a biochemical boost to men doing heavy work at high altitude. The Spanish learned that if they provided coca leaf to the miners, the men worked longer hours and ate less. The mines could increase production while lowering costs. Florencio's mother had occasionally given him coca leaf to chew at the brickyards, so he was already acquainted with the chemical benefit. For Florencio, chewing coca in the mine seemed as natural as breathing. In fact, breathing itself became more natural while chewing coca.

The boy's career in underground mining was a short one: six days. A North American engineer was inspecting operations in the shaft one day and happened to see Florencio straining to push an ore-laden tram to the dumping station. The engineer immediately called the foreman. He told the man, in no uncertain terms, that young boys were not to work underground. Florencio was immediately reassigned to the sorting yard. The sorting yard employed mostly women and girls, since the work was not strenuous. It was only tedious. Sorters crushed the rock brought up from the shafts with hammers and divided the slag from tin ore, which they sent on to the foundry. Once Florencio learned to recognize what the raw mineral looked like, he had no trouble doing the sorter job. He did, however, resent spending his days with women and girls while his male colleagues worked below.

Florencio would have another encounter with the North American engineer. One day the man spotted Florencio in the sorting yard and spoke to him.

'What's your name, son?' he asked.

The question startled Florencio. No foreigner had ever spoken to him, especially a foreigner as important as the engineer. He was afraid to answer. He looked at the ground, hoping the man would go away. When he did not, the boy quietly answered, 'Florencio Colque Vallejos.'

'Tell me, why are you working in this mine?' The engineer's questions were getting harder. Florencio hesitated. Why was this man probing his personal life? Was he in some kind of trouble?

'I have no father,' he stammered.

The man pondered this a moment. 'Do you go to school, Florencio?'

'No, I work.'

From then on, Florencio worked *and* went to school. The engineer arranged for him to attend night classes and paid Florencio's fees. He even bought the boy's books and study materials. School was a rare privilege for a child of Florencio's race and circumstances. In fact, he was the first Colque from Lequepalca to enter school. Over the following 18 months, Florencio learned his letters and how to add and subtract, skills that no one in his family had ever learned. Then his job at the San Jose mine ended. With it, his formal education ended as well.

It was not his choice. One day Florencio's mother said to him, 'Son, you are going to leave the mine. Being a miner is not good. It will cause you to have a short life. We are going back to Lequepalca.'

Valentina had her own motives for returning to Lequepalca. Her sister Justina was pregnant and asked Valentina to assist at the childbirth. In spite of Valentina's help, however, the delivery went badly. No doctor or midwife was available in Lequepalca to treat Justina and, before one could be called from Oruro, she died.

Máximo Colque was understandably distraught over his wife's death. Neither he nor Valentina had expected a problem, since Justina had previously delivered two healthy sons. The eldest, Angel, was now in his teens and his younger brother, Asencio, not far behind. But Justina's newborn, also a son, was left without his mother when he needed her most. Máximo asked Valentina to

remain in Lequepalca to care for the infant. She accepted and
Máximo fixed up a small house next to his for Valentina, Máxima
and Florencio. Máximo's baby boy, whom he christened Pablo,
lived with the three of them.

Florencio worked in the fields and Valentina cared for Pablo.
By then, Florencio's uncle Casmiro had returned from his self-
imposed exile. The *patrones* pardoned him for abandoning, years
before, the job of *hacienda* shepherd and allowed Casmiro to
settle once again on the Colque homestead. Since Gregorio
Colque had worked this plot of land before his death, his son
Florencio inherited the right to continue farming it. Casmiro had
sons of his own, Froilan and Cresencio, and the three cousins
worked together farming potatoes and *quinua*.

When Pablo Colque was 18 months old, town elders came to
speak to his father Máximo.

'We think it is time for you to marry Valentina,' they said.

'Marry Valentina?' Máximo asked. 'Why should I marry
Valentina?'

'People are beginning to talk,' the elders explained. 'Look, she
has been living with you for over a year now. She is rearing your
child. Don't you think it's about time you made it legal.'

'Yes, she has been living here,' Máximo allowed, 'but she lives
in her own house. She cooks for herself. My son Asencio cooks for
me.'

Máximo's answer surprised the officials. They turned away
for a moment to talk among themselves. They realized that
probably nothing improper was going on between Máximo and
his sister-in-law. Nevertheless, they had to consider how this
arrangement looked in the eyes of the village. They told Máximo
that, unless he were prepared to evict Valentina from his property,
he would have to take her as his wife.

'We are responsible for this community,' they reminded
Máximo. 'We can't afford any scandals.'

That evening when Florencio returned from the fields,
Valentina informed him that Máximo had asked her to marry
him and she had accepted. The boy was silent for a long time. He

had noticed Valentina paying special attention to his uncle, but had not foreseen the possibility of having Máximo as a stepfather. When he spoke, he could not hide the disappointment in his voice.

'Why do you want a husband again, Mama? We are getting along just fine the way we are.'

Máxima stopped stirring the soup she was preparing for supper and turned to look directly at Florencio. 'Son, it is hard for a widow with two children to get by alone,' she said.

Florencio looked at the floor. He was feeling a little ashamed of himself. For a moment, neither one spoke. Valentina was weighing her words, wondering if her young son would be able to comprehend what she was going to say next.

'But more than the hardship, there is the temptation,' she said gently. 'When men see a woman, and they know she is alone … well, it is hard for them to respect her.'

Valentina abruptly turned back to the cooking pot. Florencio stared at her, realizing that nothing he could say or do would cause her to change her mind. A few days later, Valentina and Máximo returned from town with a document signed by the Justice of the Peace, certifying that they had been legally joined in wedlock. Valentina gathered up her few belongings and moved them next door into Máximo's house. Florencio and Máxima had a new father.

3

The Education of a Shepherd Boy

Fifteen is an important birthday for a girl in Latin America. At this age, she ceases to be a child and enters womanhood. Her family throws a big party to mark the event, inviting all their relatives and friends. Dressed in the fanciest gown her parents can afford, the young lady glides around the dance floor on her father's arm lighting 15 candles, each one held by a close friend. Before the admiring eyes of the guests, she is toasted and applauded and welcomed to adulthood. The *quinceañero* is to a young woman in South America what the Senior Prom and High School Commencement are to a North American girl, except that it is more important than both put together.

Máxima Colque Vallejos turned 15 in Lequepalca. She had no party, no fancy gown, no 15 candles and no champagne toast to mark the occasion. Nevertheless, it was an important birthday for Máxima. It would be her last.

Máxima had tuberculosis.

Because the Colques had no access to doctors, her mother did not know the cause of Máxima's coughing when her symptoms first appeared. Valentina did the best she could for the ailing child. She brewed hot, herbal teas for her daughter. While the rest of the family tended to daily chores, Valentina kept Máxima locked in the house in bed.

But the rest and herbal teas produced no beneficial effect. Máxima's condition deteriorated until Valentina decided she must consult a professional healer. She brought Dionisio Quispe, a local *curandero*, to see Máxima. Quispe used diagnostic techniques common to *curanderos* in the Andes. Spreading an *aguayo* on the ground, he placed two ancient coins in opposite corners and sprinkled a handful of coca leaves on the coloured blanket. He studied the arrangement of the leaves for some moments before delivering the verdict.

'The leaves fail me,' he said. 'This means the girl may get sicker. But don't worry, she will eventually regain her health. In the meantime, I would give her hot, herbal teas to help the cough.'

Quispe collected his fee for the consultation and left. Valentina, relieved by the diagnosis, busied herself preparing herbal tea. Florencio looked at his sister's wan face and hoped that Quispe was right about her getting better. The *curandero* was correct in saying that Máxima would get sicker. She began coughing up blood. The tuberculosis wasted no time ravaging her frail body. Only three months after she had contracted the disease, she became too ill to feed herself or perform bodily functions. Florencio and Valentina took turns staying awake at night to care for Máxima.

About 5.30 a.m. one morning, while Florencio and his mother kept their bedside vigil, Máxima groaned loudly, then lay still. The pained expression on her face faded, her breathing stopped. She was dead.

Valentina began to weep in great, long sobs. Florencio did not want to cry. He thought it unfitting for a boy his age. But Valentina's weeping soon broke his heart. He began to sob, too, first for his mother, then for his sister. His stepfather, Máximo Colque, lay on his bed across the room watching the scene, but neither he nor his own sons wept.

The family held Máxima's funeral the same afternoon. They wrapped her body in a woollen blanket and lashed it to two long poles. Two men hoisted the litter onto their shoulders and set out at a brisk pace for the Lequepalca cemetery, five miles distant. A small group of mourners followed. At the cemetery, gravediggers prepared the hole, lowered Máxima's remains into it and covered the body with dirt. No clergyman was present to speak words over the dead girl. Among the mourners, however, were persons who knew the appropriate prayers and whispered their liturgy uninterrupted during the burial. The ceremony finished and the little company returned to Máximo Colque's house. The family gave the gravediggers and those who had recited prayers a plate of roast llama for their services.

Máxima's death saddened Florencio. For the second time in his young life, he had lost a loved one. Now he had only his mother. Emotionally, the boy drew closer than ever to Valentina. At the same time, his mother drew closer to her new husband, Máximo. She was carrying his child. Valentina would eventually have two children by Máximo, Juan and Flora, to console her for the loss of Máxima.

Due to his sister's death, Florencio experienced another emotion besides sadness – fear. The boy imagined he heard footsteps pacing back and forth in front of the house at night. He was convinced that Máxima's soul was lingering there. For nearly a year, Florencio did not venture outside after dark. Much as he had loved his sister in life, he dreaded meeting her in death.

* * *

Máximo Colque was an illiterate man. He could not read a newspaper or write a letter. He could not even write his own name. Whenever he was called upon to sign a document, he inked his right thumb and affixed the print to the paper. Admittedly, Máximo signed few documents in his lifetime. Since he was a man of modest means, he did little of the kind of buying and selling that requires signed papers. Nevertheless, signing any kind of paper was always risky business for him. Because he could not read, Máximo was never sure what the paper really said.

Ignorance was one of Máximo's greatest handicaps. It condemned him always to be at the mercy of educated people – merchants, policemen, *patrones* – anyone who could decipher the secrets of written language. Some were honest, some were not. One thing was certain, none of the educated people Máximo knew were *colonos*. Nine of every ten native Americans in Bolivia were, like Máximo, illiterate.

Máximo was determined that his sons would not inherit his handicap. They would learn to read and write. He went to the *patrón* and requested funds to build a school in Lequepalca. Señor Morales listened soberly to Máximo's plea. When he had finished, the *patrón* said, 'You and your children do not need to read, Máximo. All you have to do to live well is work every day in the fields. Besides, it is against the law to teach Indians to read.'

Máximo did not know this law. He knew almost nothing about laws, except what the *patrón* told him. If such a law existed, Máximo was helpless to do anything but obey it. He and his fellow *colonos* could never change the law. Because they were illiterate, native Americans could not vote.

'Máximo, I think I need to teach you a lesson about this,' Señor Morales continued. 'I am assigning you a week of *pongo*. But first, you will get a whipping.'

Máximo detested the beating he received from the *patrón*, but not as much as he detested the *pongo*. Traditionally, the *patrón* assigned these special work details to his *colonos* as part of their rent payment. But lately the *pongo* was used more as a punishment for defiance. For his impertinent request for a school on the *hacienda*, Señor Morales forced Máximo to stay at the main house for a week, caring for the horses. That meant Máximo could not do the work that needed to be done on his own farm. He was not even allowed to go home at night to sleep. Valentina and the boys had to get along as best they could without him. Nevertheless, the punishment did not dissuade Máximo from pursuing his goal. In fact, it strengthened his resolve to see his children educated. As soon as he could find the time, he traveled to La Paz to investigate the law Señor Morales had told him prohibited Indians from learning to read. Friends in the capital introduced Máximo to political activists sympathetic to his plight. They listened with interest to Máximo's account of his conversation with the *patrón* and explained that, although land owners were lobbying the government to pass a law restricting rural education, no such prohibition yet existed. On the contrary, government was on the side of the *colonos*, officials encouraged rural education. Señor Morales had lied.

Armed with his new knowledge, Máximo returned to Lequepalca and confronted the *patrón*. He told Señor Morales he now knew what the law said about rural education and insisted that he provide a school for the families living on the *hacienda*.

'Máximo, I see you are a stubborn troublemaker,' Señor Morales answered. 'I think you are looking for problems. Be careful that all your rabble-rousing doesn't cause you to lose your land. What would you do then?'

The implication of the threat was not lost on Máximo. Because the *patrón* held legal title to his small farm, he could order him off it at any time. The interview ended. Máximo realized that badgering Señor Morales further was not only futile, it was dangerous.

On the advice of his new acquaintances in La Paz, he devised an alternate plan for establishing a school. Máximo travelled to the provincial capital of Paria and applied for authorization to open an elementary school. With local government backing for the enterprise, he visited the normal college in Toledo to recruit a teacher. Because of the prevailing animosity to native education, few students at the normal college were willing to work on a *hacienda*, but Máximo finally convinced a young professor to give it a try. Señor Colque pledged personally to guarantee the teacher's safety.

Máximo returned to Lequepalca to prepare a school house. No adequate building existed in the village to accommodate classes, nor were his neighbours willing to risk the *patrón's* displeasure and help Máximo build one. So the first school to open in Lequepalca met under Máximo Colque's own roof.

* * *

Florencio and his stepbrothers, Angel and Asencio, were excited and apprehensive the morning their new teacher assembled the handful of pupils for their first class. Máximo was the cause of their excitement. He had primed the boys by describing to them the wonderful future that awaited a young man who could read and write and do arithmetic. Señor Morales was the cause of their apprehension. They were worried that the *patrón* might find a way to shut down the little school before they had a chance to learn to read and write and do arithmetic.

Señor Morales did not shut down the school, however, and the youngsters continued to attend the classes day after day. They settled into a familiar routine, developing their own peculiar customs and standards. Like school children everywhere, they soon learned to taunt classmates who failed to meet the standards. Florencio was one who failed. One morning a few days after classes commenced, Máximo announced, 'Florencio, you are not going to school today. You must pasture the sheep.' Florencio pastured the sheep that day, and the next and the next. When at last he returned to school, the other children chided him for the absences.

Florencio suffered taunting at meal times, as well. When the students sat down together and unwrapped the lunches they brought from home, they took careful notice of what each was eating. For most, their mothers provided boiled potatoes, *chuño* and occasional cold mutton. Florencio had only toasted corn to eat. The other boys considered this poor fare and let Florencio know their low opinion of him and his lunch. Angel and Asencio did not suffer such teasing, however. Their father saw to it that they did not lack potatoes and *chuño* in their lunch parcels. Nor did the two boys miss classes. Máximo did not assign his own sons shepherd duty on school days.

Like children everywhere, the kids in Lequepalca were keen observers. They soon realized that the differences between Florencio and his stepbrothers were due to his being an orphan. They concluded that orphans were somehow defective. 'Don't pay the orphan any mind,' they said, in Florencio's hearing. 'He has no father. Nobody cares about him. He's not good for much.'

Florencio did prove that he was good for something. At recess, when they spilled out onto the football field to test each others' skills, they quickly found out that the orphan was the best player of them all. Florencio had developed football prowess during his years in Oruro playing afternoon matches with his workmates at the San Jose mine. The boys in Lequepalca quickly learned that none of them dare tease the orphan while playing football against him.

One day, the teacher asked Florencio to remain indoors at recess. When the rest of the children were gone, the professor said gravely, 'Florencio, you have a decision to make. Either you are going to study, or you are going to pasture sheep. It just won't work trying to do both. If you can't come to school every day with the rest of the children, you should quit.'

Florencio thought about his chances of complying with the teacher's ultimatum. He knew his stepfather would refuse to excuse him from his frequent shepherd duties. Máximo certainly would not take Angel and Asencio out of class to send his stepson to school. Valentina was powerless to defy the wishes of her husband, nor could she pay Florencio's tuition out of her own pocket. Much as he wanted to promise the professor that he would improve his attendance record, Florencio knew it would be a futile promise. He told the teacher that he would drop out of school.

The next day, Florencio watched from the hillside where he had led the sheep to pasture as the other boys filed into the classroom. Angel and Asencio were there for the day's instruction, as well as Florencio's three cousins, Froilan, Cresencio and Eulogio. He thought wistfully of the future and wondered what it would hold for boys who could read and write and do their arithmetic. He wished he could be one of those boys.

* * *

Although Florencio was denied instruction in the three Rs, he did receive religious education. Like all boys in Lequepalca, he was a member of the Roman Catholic Church. Christian teaching accounted for few of his religious convictions, however, because he received precious little Christian teaching. Mass was held in the church exactly twice a year, at Easter and on 29 September, Lequepalca's civic anniversary. Years later when a friend asked

Florencio about Catholicism, the only memory he could recall was of his first confession.

'We really didn't understand what we were supposed to tell the priest, except that he expected to hear plenty of mischief. So, we mostly made things up. We got together afterward to compare notes. One boy said, "I confessed to stealing ten bills out of my mother's *aguayo*." Another one, "I told him I had a girlfriend and we had done immoral things together." We decided that, even though we had never done such things, it was maybe a good idea to confess them now while we had the chance, just in case we did commit errors later on.' The morning after confession, Florencio and his friends participated in their first communion, trying to control their giggling through the solemn Latin rite. The mass was so different from anything they had ever before experienced that they understood nothing of its significance.

In spite of their frivolous reaction to Catholicism, Florencio and his companions did hold religious convictions. They learned from their elders about good and evil. By their early teens, boys in Lequepalca were acutely aware of spiritual forces which vied for men's souls. For this instruction, Florencio was indebted to Máximo Colque's father, Dionisio. The old man had no experience with books or schools. Nevertheless, Dionisio had progressed far beyond most men in the ancient traditions of his forebears. One day Florencio watched Dionisio butcher a llama. Before he plunged the knife into the animal's throat, the old man implored in his booming voice, 'Chuquercamiri Bernita, I beg you to look upon me with favour and help me never to be without llamas to butcher.' The supplication captivated Florencio. At the first opportunity, he asked Dionisio to explain its significance. The elderly gentleman recounted this legend.

A young man was on his way home from the tropical *jungas* with his father's horse. He awoke one morning to find the horse gone. The fellow could not return home without the valuable animal, so he spent an entire day searching for it. Late in the afternoon, he came upon a lovely village nestled on the side of a mountain. The inhabitants were dressed in festive clothing. A band of musicians played enchanting melodies and the whole town danced beneath a golden sun. Best of all, the young man saw his horse tethered at the village church.

The fellow approached the horse and began to untie it. Just then a young woman, startlingly beautiful, came out of the church and greeted him.

'Is this your horse?' she asked in a voice sweet as music.

'Yes it is,' the young man answered shyly. 'Where did you find him?'

Without answering the question, the beautiful lady said, 'I would like you to bring me two cartons of candles for my church with this horse. Will you do that for me?'

'O-of course,' he stammered. 'It's, er, the least I can do for you for helping me find him.'

'Please take this for your trouble,' Chuquercamiri Bernita said, offering him a sack that appeared to contain several fat ears of corn. Without bothering to open the bag, he slung it over the pack saddle, stuttered assurances that the candles would be delivered as soon as he could manage, and said goodbye to the bewitching beauty.

When the fellow returned home, he had to explain to his father and brothers why he had been delayed and where he had acquired the extra cargo. His family was sceptical that his story was true, so he said, 'I swear to you that I am telling the truth. Look, here is the corn that Chuquercamiri Bernita gave me.'

He emptied the sack on the ground before his father. The astonished men saw that it contained not corn, but nuggets of pure gold. The miracle, of course, caused a great stir among the villagers. Soon the men of the town had loaded every available horse with candles and set off to find Chuquercamiri Bernita. None of them succeeded. The young man who received the gold also set off for Chuquercamiri Bernita's village with his two cartons of candles, intending to deliver them to her as he had promised. But as he neared the place where he knew the town must be, he found only an empty mountainside. Thinking he had mistaken the way and that Chuquercamiri Bernita must be near, he climbed over the next ridge. Again he saw only empty land. For many days he continued his vain search for the lovely village and its charming mistress. But if they still existed, they eluded him completely.

Exhausted and disappointed the young man returned home and told his father the story of his fruitless search. 'Why could I not find Chuquercamiri Bernita?' he puzzled. 'I really wanted to give these candles to her.'

The old man was well-versed in such matters. After pondering the case for a bit, he replied, 'It is clear to me that Chuquercamiri Bernita is a powerful witch who can see into men's souls. In you, she saw an innocent man who was sincere in his desire to fulfil his promise. That is why she gave you the gold. However, when the rest of the villagers went to seek her out, she saw this too. She knew their greed would mean trouble for her and her village. So she bewitched all of you so that you could not find the town.'

The news spread about Chuquercamiri Bernita and her gold. As well, word spread that only those persons of unimpeachable innocence would ever be able to find the wondrous lady and her village. People continued to hope that, perhaps if they were very, very good and tried not to think greedy thoughts, someday, maybe ...

The legend had a curious conclusion that revealed something more about Chuquercamiri Bernita. It happened that she became pregnant. Her village happily awaited the birth, hoping for a worthy successor to their charming mistress. But when time came for Chuquercamiri Bernita to deliver, what came forth was not a lovely child, but a hideous snake. The villagers' initial shock turned to disgust when they learned that Chuquercamiri Bernita was rearing the viper in a crock in her house.

One night the villagers decided to purge their town of this shameful creature. They stole to Chuquercamiri Bernita's home, uncovered the crock, doused the snake with kerosene and ignited it with a match. The cursed creature burned to ashes. The execution, however, aroused Chuquercamiri Bernita's wrath. The next morning a lone traveller chanced upon the spot and found the entire village in ashes. The bodies of the inhabitants smouldered among the ruins of their once fine houses.

When Dionisio Colque finished recounting the legend of Chuquercamiri Bernita, Florencio did not ask him how the enchantress could be both good and evil at the same time. She was, like other goddesses in other stories, fashioned of the same stuff as human beings. Florencio knew that both good and evil existed within the same human. Some nights, the boy lay awake thinking about Chuquercamiri Bernita. He hoped someday to meet the beautiful enchantress, and yearned to be found innocent and sincere.

* * *

A few days after Florencio quit school, Máximo Colque assigned him a task that caused him great excitement.

'Florencio, you are going to accompany my father, Dionisio, on a trip to Cuti Bancarani. He is going there to buy corn for us and will need your help.'

The assignment excited Florencio because it meant a long trek through the Andes, a true adventure for a boy his age. The chance to be alone with Dionisio for several days thrilled him even more. Dionisio had become like a father to Florencio, replacing the one he had lost to the plague. The bond grew to the point that, despite his adoptive status, Florencio called Dionisio, 'Grandfather'.

The two began preparing for the trip one week in advance. They butchered a llama, cut the meat into thin strips, rubbed it with salt and hung it in the sun for five days to dry. The dried llama meat, *charki* as it was called, was lightweight, durable and nutritious, an ideal food for trekking. To supplement the *charki*, Dionisio and Florencio prepared 25 pounds of *pito*. They toasted whole-grain barley in an earthen crock over a slow fire. When crisp, they ground the toasted barley into flour. *Charki*, *pito*, some

potatoes and cornmeal were all the Colques needed to feed
themselves during the three-week excursion.

Once on the trail, Dionisio and Florencio arose every morning
at dawn and breakfasted on handfuls of *pito*, washed down with
herbal tea. A bowl of cornmeal soup flavoured with a chunk of
charki topped off the morning meal. At midday they mixed *pito*
in cold water with sugar for a quick lunch. Upon completing 20
miles or so, they would stop for the night, stake out the animals
to graze and then settle down to a real meal of hearty soup, grilled
charki and boiled potatoes.

Supper finished, Dionisio would continue Florencio's religious
instruction, recounting the legends upon which the Andean peoples formed their worldview. One such legend involved Calistía,
a place the Colques passed on their way to Cuti Bancarani. At
Calistía, shadowy caves perforated huge rock formations jutting
from the mountainside. Florencio enjoyed exploring their mystery. He was careful, though, not to stray too far inside the
caverns. According to legend, they had once been enchanted.
Dionisio told him the story while they camped at Calistía.

Once a young shepherdess, who had just attained the impres-
sionable age of 13, returned home at the end of the day in a
state of ecstasy. She told her parents in breathless tones about
a wonderful gentleman she had met while pasturing sheep at
Calistía. The man had turned aside from his journey, which no
doubt was of great importance, to sit with her on the grass and
chat. He talked of the most pleasant things and shared apples
and oranges with her, treats the maiden enjoyed scarcely once
a year.

The incident amused the girl's parents, who assumed that
their gullible teenager was exaggerating about the encounter.
But when she returned the next afternoon with the same story,
and the next, and the next, their amusement changed to
concern. They told their daughter not to talk with this
stranger anymore. It was obvious that he meant some kind of
mischief. To see that she heeded the advice, the girl's father

followed her to Calistía the next morning. He stood on a peak some distance away and watched to see if the strange gentleman would appear and what his daughter would do if he did.

The man was totally unprepared for what happened. At midday, as his daughter sat tending the sheep, a huge bull drew near and stood in front of her. His appearance was terrifying. Hot vapour poured from his nostrils, sparks flew from his swishing tail. As the massive head wagged from side to side, the sun glinted off horns of burnished gold. The horrified father watched in dismay as his daughter approached the bull. He thought the beast would certainly gore her to death. But the bull stood still in its tracks. The girl began patting his massive flanks and rubbing his nose. The bull remained calm and unflinching. The girl's father, not wishing to excite the beast, remained on the distant mountaintop and kept vigil through the long afternoon. To his great relief, his daughter finally gathered the sheep and started home. The bull made no move after her.

The father arrived at home still trembling and awaited his daughter. She came in with the sheep, whistling and singing a merry tune. He threw his arms around her and wept.

'I'm so glad that no harm came to you today at Calistía,' he sobbed. 'I was terrified that huge bull would attack you at any moment.'

The maiden stared at him, thoroughly puzzled. 'What bull?' she asked. 'What are you talking about?'

Her father explained that he had followed her to Calistía and described all that he had seen from afar. But the young girl only became more and more perplexed.

'I saw no such bull today,' she said. 'Only the fair gentleman came to me there. He brought apples and oranges and shared them with me, as usual.'

Her father stared, mouth agape. Slowly it became clear to him what was happening. He spoke sternly to his daughter.

'Child, you are never to go to Calistía again. You have been bewitched by an evil spirit that is seeking to steal you away.

You think he is a fine gentleman, but that is only his disguise. I saw him for what he really is. You must never go near that place again.'

'As you say, father,' the teenager replied quietly. But in her mind, she dismissed his admonition as a jealous over-reaction to her harmless visits with the gentleman. The girl obeyed her father's instructions for a few days, thinking he might be following her, and led her flock to pastures far from Calistía. But her affection for the gentleman and her longing to taste his apples and oranges finally lured her back to the huge rocks and caverns. It was her last visit.

Since no living soul was present that day to see what happened to the shepherdess, no one ever knew exactly what befell her. But old men familiar with Calistía and its spells guessed that the spirit bull lured the maiden to the mouth of an enchanted cave among the rocks. As she stood directly in front of the cavern, a sudden wind erupted from below the earth and sucked her into the spirit bull's lair. This theory gained support when, some time later, the young maiden's sandals surfaced in a spring that bubbled out of the mountain in Colquiri, a village on the opposite side of the mountain range from Calistía.

Florencio and other boys his age were safe playing at Calistía, however. The spirit bull had long since been exorcised from the caves. Early in the colonial era, local inhabitants beckoned Catholic priests to the place to drive out the evil demon. Misfortune like that which befell the young teenager had claimed other victims at Calistía. Residents entreated the Christian fathers to expel the demon bull from the caves. The priests armed themselves with a crucifix, a Bible and a long rope and prepared themselves with prayers. When all was ready, one brave clergyman tied an end of the rope around his waist and approached the mouth of the evil cave. With Bible and crucifix held high, and with a corps of sturdy men anchoring the other end of the rope, the priest stood at the cavern mouth and rebuked the spirit within.

The priests carried the day. Once the words of exorcism had been spoken, bystanders saw a huge, golden bull burst forth from the cave and gallop away to the north. He fled to the peak of Amotar and lived on that isolated mountaintop for many years. Sightings of the beast were reported from time to time, but no one from the vicinity of Amotar ever disappeared . Thus, the wise old men who knew concluded that the spirit bull was stripped of his mystical powers at the same instant he was expelled from Calistía.

Florencio had never himself seen a real demon. He nevertheless believed in their existence as naturally as he believed in rivers and caves. This belief was reinforced by personal experience. Once Florencio set off alone on a trek. He had proved himself a capable traveller on trips with his grandfather so the family sent him with a small cargo of kerosene to Caranavi to trade for a load of barley. The signs indicated pleasant weather and Florencio started his trip confidently. The second day, however, clouds blew in and by nightfall the sky was filled with angry thunderclouds. Not wanting to be caught in the open, Florencio prodded the burro down the trail long after sunset, hoping to find shelter from the impending downpour. But rain started falling before he could reach a dry haven. For a time, he withstood the rain, protected as he was by a wide-brimmed hat and thick poncho. But when lightning began to strike close at hand, Florencio panicked. Thunder was the noise Saint James made when riding the storms clouds atop his fearsome charger. Lightning struck each time the great horse gouged the earth with its iron hoofs. The boy searched desperately for shelter to hide under before Saint James's galloping steed squashed him.

At last, a low building loomed out of the darkness ahead. Florencio could barely make out its shape in the inky blackness. His hands groped around the walls but could discover no entrance. He did find that the side opposite the wind was sheltered and dry, so he lay down close to the wall, panting from fright and ex-haustion. He soon fell asleep. When he awoke next morning, Florencio rubbed the sleep from his eyes and looked around him in the grey light of dawn. Suddenly a sickening horror overcame him. Florencio saw that he was sitting in the middle of a graveyard. The low building he had slept next to all night was a tomb.

The terrified boy leaped up from his resting place. He knew well that spirits of the dead killed intruders who disturbed their slumber. Florencio sprinted from the graveyard before the dead could attack. The fact that he was still alive at all could mean only one thing. The blessed Virgin of Copacabana had protected him in the night. As he ran, his fright slowly subsided. When he was a safe distance from the graveyard, the boy sank to his knees and thanked the Virgin for saving his life.

* * *

Many other supernatural forces were at work in Florencio's homeland, although he was not aware of them.

In Sucre, a Catholic nun, newly arrived from a journey, needed help carrying her luggage. She encountered a Quechua-speaking man on the street and asked him for assistance. The man cheerfully complied, seeing that she arrived at the convent with all her possessions safely intact. Impressed with his chivalry, the nun asked the man's name.

'I am Cirilo Lopez, sister.'

'Well, Señor Lopez, I would like to repay you for this kindness. Is there a favour I can do for you?'

Cirilo thought for a moment. 'Yes, there is something,' he said. 'I have always wanted a Bible. Would you help me get one?'

The nun promised that she would. A few days later, Cirilo answered a knock at his door and found the nun there holding a huge, leather-bound book. Trembling with excitement, she presented it to Cirilo. 'You are not to tell anyone where you got this Bible,' she cautioned. 'Should the diocese find out that I am distributing its expensive Bibles so freely, there could be a problem.'

Cirilo prized his new Bible more than any other possession. The volume contained full-page colour drawings and Cirilo enjoyed gazing at the lovely artwork. When he began to read the text, the ideas he encountered there far surpassed the sketches in beauty and power. Cirilo gradually came to realize from his reading that the Christianity he had learned from childhood differed from the Christianity his Bible revealed. At the heart of the incongruity stood the person of Jesus. Cirilo had been taught to regard Jesus as a lifeless symbol, an image to be venerated at processions. This Jesus had no personality *per se*, other than his meekness, and made few demands upon his followers. How different was the Jesus Cirilo read about in the four Gospels. His virility startled Cirilo. His simple, down-to-earth teaching intrigued him. And Christ's demand for total allegiance troubled him. Cirilo concluded that there was more to Christianity than he had so far discovered. About that time, his employer, Bolivia Federal Petroleum Reserves, transferred Cirilo to their plant in Oruro.

In Oruro, in 1944, a small band of immigrants arrived from Chile. They did not come to work in mining or commerce, however. Calling themselves 'Pentecostals', they announced that they had come in obedience to God. He had told them to start a church in Oruro.

Calixto Leon and his young wife, Catalina, lived in a modest house on Cañada Strongest Street. In the same street, Doña Consuelo operated her house of prostitution. As Providence would have it, the Pentecostals chose Cañada Strongest Street as the base for the work God had called them to do in Oruro. They began holding thrice-weekly meetings in the Leon's living room. Attendance was sparse but the listeners' interest keen. Calixto and Catalina soon embraced the new faith.

One Sunday, Cirilo Lopez, who had recently moved to town, attended the meeting. To his surprise, he discovered that the ideas about Jesus and the gospel that the Pentecostals preached closely resembled the conclusions he had reached from reading his Bible. He continued to attend the services. The more he learned of the gospel according to the Pentecostals, the more he was convinced it was true. He soon joined Calixto and Catalina in converting to the evangelical faith.

In spite of the conversions, however, a church did not form on

Cañada Strongest Street as the Pentecostals planned. In 1945, they abruptly returned to Chile. The Leons had two baby daughters, Isabel and Julia, and Calixto and Catalina felt that their growing family responsibilities took precedence over their involvement in the church. Cirilo Lopez married and returned to Sucre with his new bride. Weekly church meetings on Cañada Strongest Street ceased.

In La Paz, Luciano Condori became a Christian. Some time after his conversion, Luciano became disenchanted with the teachings of the small, Aymara-speaking church he attended. He determined to seek out a person better qualified to guide him in the fundamentals of his new faith. One night as Luciano lay dreaming, God spoke to him. The message was a name: Homer Firestone. It seemed that Luciano was to seek out this man.

In 1948, Luciano met a young missionary newly arrived in Bolivia from the United States. When Homer Firestone introduced himself, Luciano exclaimed, 'You are the one God told me to find!' The two men became close friends. For the next 16 years, they worked together as evangelists, preaching in the streets of La Paz, teaching Bible lessons in villages on the Altiplano and planting evangelical churches.

These events took place in three different cities and involved persons whom Florencio Colque had never met. Nevertheless, they would someday alter his life. God was preparing a net for his feet. In the fullness of time, he would draw the cords together, the trap would spring and Florencio and his loved ones would fall captive.

4

Soldiers

9 April 1952 was a special day in Lequepalca, Good Friday. *Colonos* did not have to work for the *patrón* on holidays. Máximo Colque took advantage of his free day and left early that morning for Oruro. He planned to buy oranges and peaches for his family to celebrate Holy Week. Florencio waited expectantly for his stepfather to return. But instead of peaches and oranges, Máximo brought news. Big news. Frightening news. Máximo trembled as he described to the family what he had seen in the city.

'They are fighting in Oruro. The miners and the university students have attacked the army. There are bodies everywhere. In the streets, in the plazas, even in the doorways of the houses. I could not reach the market. I doubt that the vendors are there today, anyway.'

'The people are very angry at the government,' he continued. 'They are shouting, "Down with the Ring!"'

The 'Ring' that the miners and the students sought to bring down represented three forces that dominated Bolivia: the *patrones*, the mine owners and the military. Throughout much of the country's history, the government had existed primarily to serve the interests of those three groups. Politicians, elected and paid by the affluent upper classes, were expected to perpetuate an economic system that favoured the Ring. The fundamental principles of the system were simple. In order to earn large profits, mine owners paid their workers dismally low wages. The *patrones* who sold food to the miners, earned large profits because they paid no wages at all to the *colonos* who worked their lands. The military policed the miners and *colonos*, preventing them from striking against their employers for better wages and working conditions. The Ring was an effective alliance that protected the interests of mining companies and *patrones* and kept the workers in their place. The Ring had made a few people rich, as well, concentrating 90 per cent of Bolivia's wealth in the hands of 5 per cent of the population.

Not all of Bolivia's leaders were part of the Ring. Occasionally, politicians appeared who wanted to overhaul the system. A few were able to rise to positions of power. That had last happened in 1943 when Gualberto Villaroel, supported by young reform-minded army officers, seized the presidency through a *coup d'état*. Despite using undemocratic tactics to take office, Villaroel did seek to build a more democratic Bolivia. He introduced reforms such as labour unions for miners and a five-day working week for *colonos*.

Villaroel's experiment in social change ended in dismal failure, however. In 1946, his opponents overthrew him in another *coup*. The deposed president's enemies shot him to death in his office and hung his body from a lamp post in the main plaza of La Paz. Villaroel's brutal murder was a message to other, like-minded, 'communistic' reformers. The Ring would allow no tampering with the system.

Following Villaroel's fall, a rapid succession of *de facto* presidents loyal to the Ring governed the country. But in 1951, the pressure of pubic opinion obliged the dictators to hold a general election. The voters rejected the Ring's hand-picked candidates. Victor Paz Estenssoro, a former cabinet minister to Gualberto Villaroel, won the presidency. The Ring did not surrender easily. General Hugo Ballivian, the acting president, refused to allow Paz Estenssoro to assume office. Ballivian's heavy-handed tactic backfired, however. Desire for democracy had been fermenting in the country and now it exploded into armed rebellion.

The fighting lasted exactly three days. By Easter Sunday 1952, miners, college students, policemen and shopkeepers had routed the Bolivian army. Indeed, most of the army were but green recruits from the countryside. The youngsters laid down their guns and refused to fight when they realized their superiors were ordering them to shoot their own cousins and uncles. During the final stage of the battle, the army officers who still survived fled the country.

With the military arm of its alliance destroyed, the Ring found itself fatally crippled. Without a loyal army to keep the workers in line, mining monopolies and *haciendas* were doomed. The Ring's end came swiftly. Late in 1952, the new government issued a decree nationalizing the country's three largest tin mining operations. The move stripped wealthy mine owners of their business empires and the political influence that went with them. The 'Tin Barons' would no longer dictate government policy in Bolivia.

The *patrones* met their *coup de grâce* on 3 August 1953. President Paz went to Ucureña, a village near Cochabamba, and signed into law the National Agrarian Reform Service. The bill dismantled all *haciendas* larger than 1,500 acres. Landlords were forced to surrender title to their properties to the government in exchange for treasury bonds. The government, in turn, deeded *hacienda* lands to the *colonos* who tended them. One hundred and fifty thousand *colonos* were present in Ucureña that day to witness the signing of the National Agrarian Reform. They celebrated their emancipation with *chicha* and dancing. For them and their children, the world had changed forever.

* * *

One of the changes altered the Bolivian vocabulary. The tenant farmer was not to be called a *'colono'* anymore because of the word's association with colonialism. Neither was *'indio'* an acceptable term. It had become a racial slur. The politically correct term from now on would be *campesino*, a person of the *campo*, the rural countryside.

As other *patrones* had done, the Morales brothers abandoned their *hacienda* in Lequepalca and moved to Oruro. Most of the cultivated acres they owned reverted to the new farmers' union. The union elected officials from among its members to manage the fields. Now instead of receiving orders from the *patron*, the *campesinos* themselves decided what they would grow and when they would grow it. In addition to cultivated land, the union received rights to the grazing range surrounding Lequepalca. Members could use pasture land free of charge. They were also free of the year-long obligation to shepherd the *patron*'s livestock, which was divided up and sold.

Florencio Colque would vividly remember the Agrarian Reform for change that it brought about in his own life. Of all the extraordinary events surrounding the 1952 revolution, one in particular carried great meaning for him personally. Florencio became a landowner. The Reform stipulated that any person who had worked a parcel of land for more than two years could now own it. *Campesinos* could receive, virtually free of charge, legal title to the land on which they lived. Since his uncle Casmiro's return several years earlier, Florencio had been working the same 40 acres in Lequepalca his family had lived on for generations. No doubt existed that Florencio fulfilled all the requirements to own the land.

A neighbour, Jose Callata, saw to it that the 16-year-old boy's right to ownership was respected. Since Florencio was a minor living with his stepfather, Jose feared that the entire Colque tract might go to his uncle, Casmiro. To ensure that would not happen, Callata spoke up for Florencio when the provincial authorities arrived in Lequepalca to register the residents' new property titles. The authorities acknowledged the lad's right to a portion of land. However, they pointed out, he had not lived on the Colque premises for several years. In answer, Señor Callata testified that the lad had worked on the land in Casmiro's employ. The clerks accepted this as evidence in the boy's favour. However, they argued that Casmiro had a large family to feed, whereas Florencio was still a minor child. Based on these contingencies, they decided to distribute the tract equally among Florencio and his first cousins, Froilan, Asencio and Eulogio. Each received 14 acres of farmland and a portion of pasture. The authorities stipulated that Florencio's share include the house in which his father had lived.

The ruling satisfied all parties involved and the clerks prepared the documents. Florencio received title to his land and stored the papers, wrapped in newspaper, in a leather pouch that hung by the head of his bed. The papers were important to the boy for they proved that he owned the land that had sustained the Colque family for generations. These few papers in the leather pouch granted him, for perpetuity, the house his grandfather built, where Florencio had been born and in which his father had died.

* * *

Sixteen years may mean one is an underage minor in the eyes of the law, but in the eyes of Máximo Colque, 16 meant Florencio was a grown man who ought to work for a living. The family was hard up, Florencio's stepfather told him, and he would have to start carrying his own weight. Máximo knew of work in the Conde Auque mine near Chicuela Alta. He suggested Florencio look into it. The boy went to work in the Conde Auque soon afterwards.

The mine was a deep-pit wolfram operation. The work was 'labour-intensive'. Labour-intensive means that, instead of buying a machine to do the work of 20 men, the owners employed 20 men to do the work of one machine. Florencio's job was ore relay. He stood all day on a small platform hewed into the wall of the vertical shaft. Ten feet below him, another man occupied a similar platform. He passed shovel loads of rock up to Florencio, who passed it on to another man on a platform above his head. These human conveyor belts composed of six or seven men perched at intervals along the shaft moved all the mineral extracted from the mine face to the dumping station. From there it was pushed to the shaft mouth in hand trams.

Florencio's job was monotonous but the pay was decent. He could afford store-bought skirts for his mother and white flour, sugar and lard for the family. For himself, he bought trousers, rubber sandals and an occasional cigar. The job had its hazards and Florencio took precautions against accidents. Upon entering the shaft every morning, he left a tribute of coca leaf or cigarettes at the shrine of *El Tio*. He believed the donations were effective because, during his entire career at the Conde Auque, Florencio encountered the devil but once.

It happened one afternoon while he was taking a turn pushing hand trams. Halfway to the shaft entrance with a heavily loaded car, he paused for a few minutes' rest. The fatigue and 100-degree heat in the mine made him drowsy. Florencio fell asleep for an instant. The sound of wings beating the air not three feet away abruptly awakened him. Thinking a rooster had wandered into the mine, Florencio turned up his carbide lamp to get a better look. As he did, the bird – or whatever had produced the furious flapping – vanished. The incident intrigued Florencio. When he told his fellow miners about it, they shook their heads gravely. 'You had better watch yourself, Florencio. No rooster would ever come this far underground.'

'If it wasn't a rooster, then what was it?'

His companions did not answer. They only shook their heads and studied the ground.

Three days later in another part of the mine, Florencio fell asleep a second time. Again he was awakened by beating wings. This time he also experienced a splitting headache. It felt like someone was trying to chisel his way out of Florencio's skull. When fellow workers found him, the young man was babbling incoherently. As they approached to help him, Florencio started screaming profanity at them. One miner tried to help him to his feet. Florencio assaulted him with flailing fists. The miners finally subdued the boy, but he continued to struggle and curse and challenge them to a fight. His co-workers carried Florencio to his quarters, dumped him on his bunk and locked the door.

When weeks of bed rest failed to restore Florencio to his senses, the boy's family brought a *curandero* to his bedside. After listening to a description of Florencio's malady, the folk doctor administered the treatment he thought appropriate. Taking a pinch of earth from the mouth of the mineshaft, he mixed it in coca water and forced Florencio to drink it. For 24 hours, the *curandero* spoke incantations over Florencio, rebuking the spirits that were tormenting him. To the chants he added sacrifices. Two roosters were slaughtered and their blood sprinkled on the mine entrance. The *curandero* then prepared a fire and burned the dead roosters, along with a dried llama fetus. 'I burn the animals so you will be saved from the flames,' the *curandero* explained to Florencio.

Two weeks later, Florencio had recovered from his illness. Valentina Colque was sure the *curandero*'s treatment had saved her boy's life. She gratefully delivered sacks of *quinua* and *chuño* to the folk doctor. Florencio returned to shovelling wolfram at the Conde Auque mine.

After 18 months at the mine, the boy decided, with the help of his stepfather, that the time had come to enter the army. Like every able-bodied 18-year-old male in Bolivia, Florencio was required to perform one year's military service. His eighteenth birthday was still some months away but that presented no problem. Florencio simply went to a notary public and bribed the man to change the date on his birth certificate.

* * *

Basic Training: A three-month period in which the Bolivian Army attempts to turn teenage farm boys into dependable soldiers.

Order of the Day: 6 a.m. Reveille. 7 a.m. Barracks swept and inspected. 7.30 a.m. Breakfast. 8 a.m. Instruction. 12 noon Lunch. 1 p.m. Work detail. 6 p.m. Supper. 7 p.m. Specialty class. 10 p.m. Lights out.

Soldiers' Mess: *Sultana* tea made with coffee bean husks and cornmeal *lawa*. Three times a day. For flavour, army cooks occasionally added goat meat to the *lawa*. For bravery, the cooks occasionally added dog meat.

The recruits never actually ate dog meat. The mess sergeant only allowed them to see the head simmering in the pot. If anyone asked, he was told that dog imparted aggressiveness to the soldiers. Cooks sometimes added kerosene to the *sultana* tea. Some said this also imparted aggressiveness. Others speculated that it helped suppress libido. Many believed the kerosene cured the recruits' most common malady – homesickness. The first nights of basic training, Florencio lay in his bunk listening to other soldiers cry themselves to sleep. They wept for their mothers, their brothers and sisters, their homes. 'Drinking kerosene in your tea will forge character,' he heard the sergeant say. 'We will turn you sissies into men.' Florencio drank his *sultana* and gradually the yearning for his home and family back in Lequepalca subsided.

Whether or not the kerosene cured his homesickness, Florencio believed it produced a beneficial effect on his digestive system. Like most *campesinos*, he was infected with parasites from childhood. Once his intestinal tract absorbed the kerosene, however, the amoebas and round worms found the environment less hospitable. His system purged of the bugs, Florencio began to gain weight.

Daily calisthenics were not so rigorous for the ex-miner as for the city boys. Shovelling ore had developed the muscles required for push-ups, sit-ups and jumping jacks. At the close of each morning's drill, the recruits duckwalked around the parade ground, their rifles balanced across their shoulders. Florencio typically finished at the head of the line. In the afternoons, manual labour occupied the young soldiers. They built barracks, officers' quarters, roads, whatever the army needed. The army needed quite a lot in those days. Bolivia's armed forces were nearly destroyed by the Revolution of 1952 and the military was short on money, manpower and material.

From the outset of their military career, the recruits learned the army's code of discipline. Offences were classified as minor or grave. Minor offences included sleeping past reveille, failing to salute an officer or personal sloppiness. The code was easy to understand and recall, even for soldiers who spoke no Spanish, because officers constantly gave them object lessons. Drill sergeants punished minor offences with a forceful kick to the seat of the pants and ordered the offender to do extra calisthenics. A recruit who committed a grave offence such as picking a fight, losing his rifle or getting drunk while on duty, merited a serious penalty which was imposed by a lieutenant. If the soldier was on friendly terms with the officer, he might get off easily, say, with all-night guard duty. Otherwise, he suffered the full force of the code. A common penalty was to tie six or eight rifles or, perhaps, a truck tyre to the soldier's back and order him to march, double-time, around the parade ground perimeter. The march lasted all morning. Two soldiers armed with switches jogged along beside the offender. They were under orders to whip him when he tired and stopped to rest.

Florencio completed three months of basic training without a single grave offence on his record. He was finding army life tolerable, even though he had been stationed on the Argentine border and had no chance to visit home during his brief periods of liberty. To ease his loneliness, Florencio signed up for a literacy class. He applied himself diligently to the studies and soon was writing letters to his family back in Lequepalca. He did not expect to receive any reply, of course, but he was glad to be able to communicate with his parents so they would not worry about him. A corporal, a boy from the city who knew how to use the post office, collected the recruits' letters and postage money each week and mailed the correspondence.

One morning Florencio's unit was washing their laundry at the river and spreading the wet clothes over bushes to dry. Under one of these bushes the soldiers discovered a concealed cache of unposted letters, addressed to their families. They carried the weather-beaten letters to the sergeant and explained that the corporal evidently had been pocketing their postage money. The sergeant immediately informed the post commander who ordered the corporal's arrest. Under questioning, the young man admitted his offence. The charge was grave: fraud committed against comrades in arms. The commander decided to make an example of the con artist.

The entire post formed up around the parade ground perimeter to witness the punishment. The corporal was stripped to his underclothes and made to lie prostrate on the ground. Two soldiers held him down, one by the arms and one by the feet. An officer administered 20 lashes with a bull whip. During the opening minutes of the beating, the offender screamed and begged for mercy. Then he lost consciousness and the screaming stopped. The punishment duly administered, soldiers carried the corporal to the infirmary. He required two weeks of bed rest to recover from the whipping.

Despite the disheartening outcome of this first attempt, Florencio continued to write letters. He noticed that literacy was key to advancement in the army. All the officers were educated men. An enlisted man's success in climbing the ranks correlated with the amount of schooling he had. Florencio figured the same principle must operate in civilian life, as well. Besides learning his letters, he continued to develop his football skills and was selected for the post team. As a military athlete, Florencio travelled to bases in Tupiza, Tarija and Uyuni to compete in matches. The trips provided a welcome change from the drudgery of drills and work details. His ability on the football field soon paid greater dividends. Near the end of his tour of duty at Villazón, Florencio's unit was mustered out on the parade ground one morning to hear a special announcement from the commanding officer.

'Any of you men who are originally from La Paz take one step forward,' he ordered. No one moved.

'Good,' the commander said. 'Now any of you who are football players, take one step forward.' After a moment of hesitation, Florencio and his teammates obeyed.

The commander reviewed the contingent carefully for a few moments. Satisfied by the brief survey, he announced, 'You men pack your gear and get ready to leave for La Paz tomorrow morning. The army needs you to play football.'

Fortune had smiled on Florencio. He spent the remaining months of his tour of duty in the capital. Army life there was better in every respect than in Villazón. Football practice occupied most of the morning, freeing him from drills and work details. He enjoyed much more liberty than he had been allowed at Villazón and used it to see the sights of La Paz. Military athletes enjoyed other perks. Uniforms issued to the football team were new, not faded and patched like the ones they had worn at their former post. The food was better, too. *Lawa* was still a standard fare, but Florencio and his teammates no longer ate it three times a day. For breakfast, they got bread and tea, real tea not *sultana*. Beef and mutton were regular features at other meals, as was *mote*, a favourite corn dish, and *quinua*. By now, Florencio was virtually enjoying army life. When officers invited him to extend his tour, he signed up for an additional six months.

The decision was prompted more by his love of football than of the military, however. The thrill of his new surroundings eventually wore thin. Life settled into a predictable routine and his enthusiasm diminished. In private moments, Florencio found himself thinking more and more about his family. Barracks life was tolerable but it was not home. The sights of La Paz were interesting but not familiar. When his extra six months were up the lad requested his discharge papers and headed for Lequepalca on the first train he could catch.

* * *

Bolivia attracts fewer foreign tourists than any country in South America but those who do come almost always visit Tiahuanacu. A thousand acres of stone ruins lying under the soil of the Altiplano near the shores of Lake Titicaca are all that remains of the ancient city. Archaeologists believe Tiahuanacu was the largest metropolis on the continent in its day and the centre of a highly advanced culture that stretched for hundreds of miles north to south. Though not nearly as large as the later Inca empire, the Aymara-speaking Tiahuanacu civilization bequeathed many of its secrets to the Incas. For one, Tiahuanacu taught the builders of Cuzco how to carve massive stones into splendid building blocks for palaces and temples. As well, the ancient Aymaras also inspired the priests of Machu Picchu to study the heavens and trace the movements of stars, moon and sun.

One secret that Tiahuanacu has revealed to no one, however, is how it came to be. Researchers have managed to excavate only about 15 of its 1,000 acres, so little is known about the origin of the great stone city. It seems, however, that Tiahuanacu arose in a relatively short period of time contemporaneous with the advent of Christianity. What motivated the Aymara people to undertake city building at that point in history baffles anthropologists. Nor can they explain how the builders constructed Tiahuanacu with such remarkable precision. The mystery has led one writer to speculate that extraterrestrials erected the ancient city, quarrying its huge stones with laser beams and transporting them to the building site in spaceships.

Tiahuanacu disappeared, just as mysteriously as it arose, sometime in the twelfth century AD. Archaeologists have yet to explain why this robust civilization disintegrated just at that point in history, again in an uncommonly brief time span. No evidence suggests that a rival army destroyed the city. If plague slew its inhabitants, no record of the epidemic has reached us. For want of a better explanation, tour guides at Tiahuanacu tell visiting tourists that a geological cataclysm destroyed the place. One version has it that a meteor struck the Altiplano near the Uyuni Salt Flats and sent a gigantic tidal wave of dirt northward, burying Tiahuanacu and its inhabitants as Vesuvius interred ancient Pompeii.

Wise old men in the Andes tell their grandchildren their own account of Tiahuanacu's rise and fall. Viracocha founded the city, they say, to teach the people true religion. He originally gave it the name Taipi Q'ala, which means 'The Stone in the Middle'. As the title suggests, Andean peoples consider Tiahuanacu to be a spiritual centre. In its heyday, pilgrims flocked to the city's temples and pyramids to worship the Creator God and learn Viracocha's teachings. But with the passing of the centuries, the old men say, people fell into wickedness and idolatry. They traded worship of Viracocha for allegiance to lesser gods, seeking personal prosperity and comfort in place of goodness and truth. Their apostasy angered Viracocha so he utterly destroyed Tiahuanacu. Only a remnant of its multitudes escaped and made their way to Cuzco, where they constructed the Inca empire from Aymara cultural remains.

According to the old wise men, Tiahuanacu was not the only Andean empire that suffered destruction for turning its back on Viracocha. Grandfathers tell a cryptic tale of Huayna Kapac, the last great Inca emperor and father of Huáscar and Atahualpa. These were the rival half-brothers who, after their father's death, split the empire in two and fought a debilitating war of succession. The brothers' feud set the stage for Francisco Pizarro to subdue the entire Inca world with a handful of Spanish soldiers of fortune.

One day near the end of his reign, Huayna Kapac witnessed a strange sight. A flock of small birds set upon a powerful hawk and killed it. Later, Huayna Kapac lay dying in Quito of a strange, new disease. Rumors were circulating in the Inca capital about Pizarro and his band of mercenaries. The Spaniards had briefly landed on the coast of Ecuador, then returned to Panama. Their visit had infected the native population with small pox and the illness was killing thousands of people within the empire, including Huayna Kapac. The dying emperor chose the moment to call his two sons, Huáscar and Atahualpa and tell them of the omen he had witnessed.

'Just as those small birds killed the great hawk, so a weaker enemy is going to destroy us,' Huayna Kapac prophesied. 'God is about to punish us for our sin.'

'What sin is that?' his sons asked.

'We have forgotten our true God,' Huayna Kapac said. 'We made for ourselves idols, which he abhors, and have fallen away from his laws. God has sent these men to kill you, rape your daughters and destroy our throne.'

'Remember this,' the old Inca added. 'The day you repent and love one another and turn from your idolatry, our nation will be restored.'

Evidently, neither Huáscar nor Atahualpa heeded their father's warning. After his death, political ambition led them to declare war on one another. The conflict, of course, precluded any religious reform they might have undertaken. Then, just as Atahualpa was defeating his elder brother, Pizarro arrived in the Andes. It was too late to escape the impending disaster.

Historical evidence, gleaned from Atahualpa's final days, suggests that the last Inca must have known something about the true God of which his father spoke. For one thing, he issued orders to his armies not to attack the Spaniards as they advanced from the coast toward the mountains. Perhaps, he reasoned, they were messengers of Viracocha, who had long ago left the Andes with a promise to return one day. The strangers did resemble descriptions of Viracocha. They were tall, light-skinned and bearded. As well, one of their company wore long vestments like those described in the legends. This would have been the Dominican friar, Vicente de Valverde, the first Christian missionary to arrive in Peru. If Viracocha had sent these men to his realm, Atahualpa reasoned, then they must not be harmed.

Pizarro skilfully exploited Atahualpa's hesitation. He lured the Inca emperor to the village of Cajamarca and prepared an ambush. Pizarro hid his soldiers in buildings surrounding the town plaza. They poised there with weapons drawn as Atahualpa and his royal retinue arrived, unarmed, to meet the visitors. Under orders from King Charles to use violence only as a last resort, Pizarro sent Vicente de Valverde to speak first with Atahualpa. Valverde carried a cross and a Bible. Through a Quechua interpreter, the priest expounded his Roman Catholic faith. He concluded the homily with an invitation to Atahualpa to join the great brotherhood of Christian nations and submit to the Spanish emperor, Charles I of Spain and V of Austria. The Christian Pope had commissioned Charles, Valverde declared, to eradicate paganism in the New World and establish the holy Roman and Apostolic Catholic Church in its place.

Atahualpa responded by asking Valverde where he had learned this story. Valverde said that it was all contained in the Bible he held in his hand. Atahualpa had never seen a book before, nor did he understand that language could be represented in writing. He asked Valverde's Quechua interpreter how this Bible could tell the priest so many things. The man said, 'God speaks to him in the book.'

Atahualpa took the Bible from Valverde and held it to his ear. Hearing nothing, he tossed the book on the ground in disgust. 'If your God is in there, he must be very small,' he said to the priest. 'My God can hold the universe in his hand.'

The Inca's desecration of the sacred book and his refusal to accept the Catholic faith convinced Valverde that he was dealing with a hardened infidel who would never willingly convert to Christianity. The priest turned away and signalled to Pizarro and his men to commence the attack.

5

True Believer

The train creaked and groaned through the night and Florencio shivered in the empty wagon. Icy wind blew in through cracks in the walls and penetrated the heavy woollen blanket he had wrapped around himself. It was July, the coldest month on the Altiplano; 4 a.m., the coldest hour of the night. Florencio built a fire in the corner of the old wagon, but it proved a poor defence against the chill. He would have felt miserable except for the fact that this was his last train ride as a soldier. He was on his way home to Lequepalca with discharge papers in his pocket certifying that he had honourably completed military service. These were the papers that every young man in Bolivia needed in order to get a job or be married or secure a passport. These were the papers that guaranteed full adult citizenship to Florencio Colque Vallejos.

The young ex-soldier was thinking about the little house by the river where his mother and stepfather were waiting for him. He hoped that they would be waiting. He had not seen them for the entire year and a half that he had spent in the army, nor had he received messages from them in that time. If one of them had died in the past 18 months, Florencio would find out upon his arrival at home. Though it was still dark when the train pulled into the Oruro station, Florencio had no trouble finding his way through the familiar streets. His stepbrother Angel had moved to town to take a job with Bolivian Federal Petroleum Company so Florencio headed for his apartment. He aroused Angel from sleep and asked to borrow his bicycle for the ride to Lequepalca. But Angel, pleased to see Florencio after so many months, insisted on taking his younger sibling home himself. Angel dressed and the two set off on the bicycle together. By sunrise, they were already well across the grassy plain between the city and the mountains. Florencio, perched on the handlebars, compared his army experiences with Angel.

At mid-morning they arrived in Lequepalca. The place looked as it always did in the middle of the dry season, brown and dusty from three months of no rain. Florencio approached the house and saw his mother emerge from the doorway. She recognized her son, squealed with delight and ran to embrace him. Máximo stepped out and, seeing the young man, moved sedately to where Florencio stood and shook his hand.

In honour of his return, Máximo and Valentina prepared a *watia* for Florencio. They dug a shallow hole in the ground and built a fire in it. When the coals were glowing hot, they heaped on potatoes, laid a freshly butchered lamb on top and covered the hole with earth. Although Florencio had enjoyed many *watias* in his lifetime, he decided the one his parents served that day was the best ever.

When they had finished eating, Florencio drew his stepfather aside and broached a delicate subject. He explained that he had arrived from the army post with only two pairs of pants and a shirt, all military issue. He could no longer wear these clothes in public. The law prohibited civilians from wearing military uniform. Florencio urgently needed to buy some civilian clothes. Would Máximo be able to spare a marketable lamb for him to sell? His stepfather shifted uneasily and looked off into the distance. Florencio knew his answer before it came. 'I'm sorry, Florencio,' Máximo said, 'we are a little hard up right now. There really are no lambs to sell.'

Máximo did not know that Valentina was listening to this conversation from the doorway. She said nothing to her husband about the matter but made up her mind what she would do. When Florencio awoke the next morning, his mother was not in the house. He was not worried by her absence because, during the dry season, she often left well before dawn to find pasture for the sheep. But Valentina was not pasturing sheep this morning. She had arisen from her bed at midnight. After driving the herd to a neighbour's fold, she boarded a truck bound for Oruro.

Early that afternoon, Valentina arrived at the house herding the bleating flock before her. Florencio helped her water the sheep and drive them into the corral. Then he followed his mother into the house. Once inside she untied her *aguayo*, took out of it a new suit of clothes and wordlessly presented them to her son. Florencio stared at the new clothes, then at his mother.

'How … ? What did you …?' he stammered.

Valentina put her finger to her lips in a gesture that meant 'it is best not to ask' and turned to rearrange her *aguayo*.

'There was a lamb,' she said quietly.

* * *

The monotonous rhythm of farm life was beginning to bore Florencio when potato planting rolled around that November. Once the planting season began, however, he worked too hard to be bored. He and Máximo were in the fields soon after sunrise each day turning the ground with their hoes, dropping in the seed tubers and covering the hills with dirt. They worked six days a week for a month to sow 700 pounds of seed. Then they rested and waited for the rains.

But that December, no rain fell. The farmers scanned the clear blue sky every day for signs of an approaching storm, but none ever came. It was not until after Christmas that Lequepalca received its first good drenching. This was enough to get the young plants up out of the ground by mid-January, when the farmers expected the heavy rains to fall. But that January was even drier than December. Ominously dry, and cool as well. The stunted plants were just managing to produce a few feeble blossoms when a worse disaster struck – frost. Many of the plants succumbed to the ice and withered. Amazingly some stricken plants, perhaps half, recovered from the freeze and struggled on. The effort was poorly rewarded. Through February and March the drought persisted. Some days clouds appeared, but passed on. Lequepalca's farmers feared the worst.

Their fears were confirmed when harvest time arrived that April. One morning, Florencio and his stepfather went out to their potato field to examine a few selected hills. They wanted to see if it would be worth digging the whole crop. They pulled up one of the spindly plants, easily extracting it from the crumbly, dry earth. Pea-size tubers, shrivelled like raisins, clung to its roots. They dug down farther with their hands, encountering more of the tiny, wrinkled potatoes. None were bigger than a thumb tip.

The Colques straightened up from their work and looked at each other mutely; 1958 was going to be a hard year for the *campesinos* in Lequepalca.

* * *

Because of the potato crop failure Florencio urgently needed to find a paying job to help the family through to the next growing season. He went back to mining, the one occupation for which he had experience. The Conde Auque mine was taking on workers and hired Florencio immediately. He found the work just as monotonous as ever but not as difficult. Nearly a full-grown man, he could easily keep up with the other miners. Mining might have become his life's career, in fact, had not the Conde Auque changed hands a few months later. The new owners decided to retool the operation so they closed the mineshaft and laid off most of the miners. Those with seniority received generous severance. Some long-term employees even took early retirement. But Florencio had not worked long enough to qualify for severance. The money he took home with him would not even buy seed for next year's potato planting.

Nevertheless, the Colques did manage to scrape together enough potato seed to sow their fields. The rains that had failed to come in 1958 fell in abundance in 1959 and there were potatoes once again in Lequepalca. Florencio, his cousins and stepbrothers worked several weeks in the fields gathering the harvest. During those days, the National Highway Service was working on the road immediately across the river from the Colque farm. The government had decided to upgrade it from a dirt track to a two-lane, gravelled highway. It fascinated Florencio to watch the dump trucks growl up and down the road, staggering under huge loads of rock and sand. One day a truck stopped where he was working and the driver called to him.

'Young man! How would you like to fill this dump truck for me with gravel from the river bottom?'

'Of course,' responded Florencio, eager for the opportunity to study the powerful truck up close. He attacked the work with a burst of energy that impressed the driver. He paid Florencio for the load and promised to come back for another. Florencio filled the truck a second time with the same dispatch. The driver realized he had a willing worker on his hands. At the end of the day, he made Florencio an offer.

'How would you like to do this for a living?'

The young man needed no time to think it over. Digging gravel was no harder than digging potatoes. The pay was not great, but it was steady. A highway job meant being around big trucks and earth movers all day. For Florencio, that was the best part. He said he would take the job. That afternoon he signed on full-time with the National Road Service. Though he could not know it at the time, he would hold the job for the rest of his working life.

* * *

Florencio used his first pay cheque from the Highway Department to take his mother to Oruro. However, they did not go to town to celebrate his new job. They went to see Dr Pastor Navia, the best physician Florencio could afford. Valentina had taken ill and the sickness turned chronic. Florencio knew she was seriously ill when, for three days straight, she was unable to rise from her bed in the morning. This was quite out of character for his mother and it worried Florencio greatly. The young doctor carefully examined Valentina, who had lost considerable weight and showed signs of jaundice. He said that he thought he knew what the disease was, but wanted to do some laboratory tests to confirm the diagnosis. This meant considerable expense for Florencio, but he told Dr Navia to go ahead with the tests.

When the results were in, Dr Navia sent for Florencio.

'These tests have confirmed my suspicions,' he began soberly. 'Your mother has developed a very serious disease. It's called cirrhosis of the liver. Very few people ever recover from it, even with prompt treatment, and your mother's illness is far advanced. Florencio, I'm sorry to have to tell you this, but your mother will die within a year.'

The news was a crushing blow to Florencio. Once orphaned, he could not bear to think of losing his only surviving parent. He did not doubt Dr Navia's diagnosis, but did resolve to try every avenue open to him to save his mother's life. If the medical doctors could offer no hope, then Florencio would take his mother to the *curanderos*.

The first one he consulted was Dionisio Quispe. The Colques brought Valentina to the man, explained her symptoms and told him what the doctor had said. Quispe listened impassively. Taking out a deck of playing cards, he spread them on the table. He carefully scrutinized the order and position of each card. After a while, he announced his decision.

'It is clear to me that your mother has a malignancy that will, in time, infect your entire family. If you want to cure your mother and avoid contracting her illness yourselves, you will have to sacrifice three black sheep.'

Florencio thought this a small price to pay for his mother's life and the rest of the family's health and entreated his stepfather to go along with Quispe's scheme. Máximo agreed to deliver the sheep.

The *curandero* gave them instructions.

'One evening this week you will butcher one of the black sheep and roast it. I will come to eat it with you. At that time you will deliver to me the two other black sheep. These I will lead to an undisclosed location where the spirits who are causing this illness to lurk. I will kill the sheep there and the illness will pass into the demons. Valentina will recover and the sickness will be prevented from coming upon the rest of you.'

This seemed like a sensible plan to the Colques. They agreed to follow Quispe's directions and also agreed to pay his fee. The charge was one white lamb to be delivered to Quispe the night he came to supper. Máximo would have insisted that payment for the man's services be withheld until Valentina showed signs of responding to the treatment. But Florencio talked Máximo out of insisting. The young man was anxious for the *curandero* to perform his services with all good will.

The evening the Colques roasted the black lamb, Quispe came as he had promised and ate it with them. After the meal, he went home leading the two black and one white sheep with him. The family did not witness what he did with the black sheep, but in a few days Valentina's health began to improve. Florencio was relieved to see the illness checked and credited Quispe with effecting her cure. But after two months of relative improvement, Valentina suffered a relapse. This time the family thought better of consulting Quispe, so they took her to another *curandero*. That man had even less success than his predecessor. The Colques then resorted to a third *curandero* but he likewise proved inept. For the next year they consulted a succession of folk doctors, but Valentina's condition steadily worsened. It appeared that Dr Navia's prognosis was correct. Valentina would die.

* * *

Angel Colque was working in Oruro at the Federal Petroleum plant while his family in Lequepalca agonized over Valentina's lingering illness. Angel had formed a close friendship with a fellow worker at the plant who was an evangelical Christian. The gentleman took Angel to worship services at a local church. Initially Angel was suspicious of the evangelicals, having been taught from childhood that their beliefs about God and the Bible were heretical. But when he heard for himself what they taught he found their beliefs quite sensible.

His relationship with the man who invited him to the church services helped convince Angel that evangelical religion was genuine. The man, nearly old enough to be Angel's father, radiated enthusiasm. He reported for work everyday smiling and humming tunes. He was knowledgeable in many interesting topics and liberally injected quotes from the Bible into his conversation. He seemed to think that the Scriptures had something to say about every aspect of life. Angel learned from the man that the Scriptures certainly had something to say about future life. His friend's explanations about heaven struck a familiar chord in Angel's thinking. He had always believed that he would continue to exist, in some form or another, after he died. He came to believe, through conversations with his friend, that what the Bible said about salvation and eternal life was true. One day, Angel decided to act upon that belief.

'I want to surrender myself to God,' he said to his friend.

'I see,' the man replied, a hint of caution in his tone. 'Tell me, Angel, what would be your motive for doing this?'

'What do you mean?' the young man asked.

'People have all kinds of motives for becoming believers,' the man explained. 'Some see their evangelical neighbours prosper after conversion. They want this new religion in order to make a better living. Others are pressured by relatives to join the faith. Still others think that believing in Christ for salvation will keep them healthy. There are all kinds of motives, but only one true one.'

'What is that?' Angel wanted to know.

'The realization that you are a sinner and that God is calling you to repent and believe in Jesus Christ.'

Angel reflected on this a moment. He could say truthfully that he had never linked the idea of becoming an evangelical with personal prosperity. In fact, many of the evangelicals he knew lived in humble circumstances. Nor had it occurred to him that conversion would grant him immunity from illness. Certainly none of his family was pressuring him to convert. On the contrary, they would probably discourage him from it, if they knew. No, he wanted to believe the gospel not for what it offered in this life but for what it promised in the life to come.

'I want to trust Christ for salvation because God is calling me,' he said.

'How long do you plan to serve him?' the gentleman asked. 'Two weeks? A month? Perhaps a couple of years? Or have you decided to follow Jesus until the final moment of your life?'

Angel considered this. 'Until the final moment, I suppose. Isn't that what he expects?'

The man smiled faintly. 'Very well, I think you understand what you are doing. Now I must ask you if you hold any grudges against anyone.'

Angel thought for a moment. 'Yes, I think I must hold some grudges. Why do you ask?'

'Because Jesus said in Matthew 6.14–15, "If you forgive men their trespasses, your heavenly Father also will forgive you; but if you do not forgive men their trespasses, neither will your Father forgive your trespasses." Before you can ask the Lord to forgive your sins, Angel, you must go to those who have wronged you and forgive them.'

Angel agreed to do this. The man was satisfied that young Colque was ready to receive Christ into his heart. To do this, he had Angel kneel, facing him. The man took a huge Bible in both hands and placed it on Angel's head. He told the young man to repeat a prayer of repentance. As they prayed, the man accentuated his words by tapping Angel on the head with his Bible, the taps becoming more forceful as the volume of the prayer increased. When Angel had finished repeating the prayer, his friend lifted both arms heavenward and implored God to accept this poor sinner into his Kingdom.

'Stand up,' he said to Angel when he had finished. The two friends shook hands and embraced. 'Welcome into the family of God,' the man said, smiling broadly. 'We are now brothers in Christ. The Bible says in 2 Corinthians 5.14, "If anyone is in

Christ, he is a new creation; the old has passed away, behold, the new has come.'"

* * *

Not long after his conversion, Angel paid a visit to his family in Lequepalca to see how his ailing stepmother was doing. He found her much worse than on his previous visit. Florencio gloomily recounted to him the list of *curanderos* they had consulted and the cures they had attempted, all to no avail. Angel immediately thought of his friend at the petroleum plant. The man, in addition to his reputation as a preacher, was also known as a healer of notable ability. Angel had been intrigued by a remark he had overheard one day at the plant. 'If you ever get sick and the doctors can't do anything for you, go to the evangelical, he will fix you up.'

Angel said to Florencio, 'I know a man at work who I am sure can help Valentina. He's an evangelical. I think he would even be willing to come out here to see her. His name is Cirilo Lopez. He's from Sucre.'

Florencio had never heard of him before, but he agreed to give the evangelical healer a try. After all, he reasoned, they had tried every *curandero* in the area and Valentina's condition continued to deteriorate. This man probably would do her no harm.

The following Sunday, Angel and Cirilo Lopez arrived at the Colque home on bicycles. After the customary introductions, Cirilo was led to Valentina's bedside for the examination. He recognized that she was in the final stages of cirrhosis. His prognosis was guarded.

'This is what we are going to do,' he said to Valentina. 'I will give you injections for your liver and pray that God will heal you. But you must understand that he will do so only if he chooses. I cannot guarantee that he will. If God does not heal you, it is clear that you are going to die. I would suggest that you prepare yourself to meet your Creator.'

To the Colques, who had heard glowing assurances from every *curandero* in the province, Cirilo's frank appraisal of Valentina's condition sounded pessimistic. They suspected that he was down-playing his possibilities for success, so that if Valentina did not get well, no one would blame him for her death. On the other hand, the family had to admit that Cirilo was being straightforward with them about the odds against her recovery. Having been disappointed so many times by sure-fire cures, the family found his honesty refreshing. Also, Cirilo required no fee for his services. The Colques found that refreshing, as well. They agreed to his terms.

Cirilo gave Valentina an injection and prayed for her, tapping her on the head with his huge Bible as he entreated the Great Physician to heal her of the cirrhosis. He promised to return with Angel the following Sunday. True to his word, Cirilo Lopez rode to Lequepalca the next week on his bicycle to see Valentina Colque. Smiling and humming tunes, he seemed unconcerned that his patient showed no apparent improvement. After giving her another injection, he produced the huge Bible, the same one he had received years before from a nun in Sucre, and turned to 2 Kings 20. As he read, he translated the story into Quechua so all of the hearers could understand.

> In those days Hezekiah became sick and was at the point of death. And Isaiah the prophet the son of Amoz came to him, and said to him, 'Thus says the LORD, "Set your house in order; for you shall die, you shall not recover."' Then Hezekiah turned his face to the wall, and prayed to the LORD, saying, 'Remember now, O Lord, I beseech thee, how I have walked before thee in faithfulness and with a whole heart, and have done what is good in thy sight.' And Hezekiah wept bitterly. And before Isaiah had gone out of the middle court, the word of the LORD came to him: 'Turn back, and say to Hezekiah the prince of my people, "Thus says the LORD, the God of David your father: I have heard your prayer, I have seen you tears; behold, I will heal you; on the third day you shall go up to the house of the Lord. And I will add fifteen years to your life."'

Cirilo laid aside his Bible and said to Valentina, 'This week as I was praying for you, the Lord reminded me of this text. What's more, he promised me that if you, Valentina, will turn your face to the wall and cry out to Him, he will heal you and add 15 years to your life.'

Valentina pondered this. What did it mean to 'cry out to the Lord', she wanted to know. Cirilo said that she and her family must surrender themselves to God and believe in Jesus Christ as saviour. Then, like King Hezekiah, they would be able to walk before God in faithfulness and with a whole heart and do good in his sight. If they would do this, God had revealed to Cirilo, Valentina would be healed of the cirrhosis.

The Colques were not eager to follow Cirilo's suggestion. Nobody in Lequepalca, except for the *curandero* Dionisio Quispe, had ever converted to the evangelical faith. They knew the community would ostracize them for their decision. Cirilo acknowledged that this could be a serious problem. On the other hand, there was one compelling reason to follow his advice. It might save Valentina's life.

As they talked over the decision, other factors in favour of the Colques accepting Christ presented themselves. One was Angel's conversion, which set a compelling precedent. They all trusted Angel's judgement. It seemed that his new faith had not adversely affected him. Secondly, there was Cirilo himself. The firmness of his faith in God and the confidence he placed in the words of his huge black Bible were real. After much discussion among themselves, the Colques finally chose to do as he said. Cirilo instructed them in the steps they must take, the same steps Angel had taken a few weeks before. They understood that this was a lifetime commitment and each promised to follow the Lord until the final moment. They agreed as a family to put away all hard feelings and took turns asking and granting forgiveness for past offences. There was weeping as they did this. Tears melted the emotional barriers that separated stepfather from stepson, a mother from her adopted children.

When the family completed their reconciliation, Cirilo had them kneel and repeat the same prayer of repentance that Angel had prayed. He then implored God to accept this poor sinful family into his kingdom. When he finished, he embraced each of them and welcomed them to the new life they had chosen in Christ. Cirilo left Lequepalca that afternoon with the promise that he would return the following Sunday to instruct the family in their new faith. He returned for many weeks, always with the huge Bible, to exhort the Colques to faith and righteousness. They heeded his message and tried sincerely to live as the Scriptures directed.

Beginning that Sunday when the Colque family surrendered to God, Valentina began to recover from the cirrhosis. Her skin lost its yellowish cast and turned a healthy bronze colour once again. She regained weight and, with it, her characteristic energy. In a remarkably short time, particularly in light of the gravity of her illness, she was back on her feet and doing her customary tasks. Within a year, no detectable sign of her cirrhosis remained.

Like Hezekiah, Valentina had been under the sentence of death. She had cried out to the Lord to spare her life. The Lord answered her cry, as he had answered the king of ancient Judah, and healed her of a fatal disease. Cirilo's prediction concerning Valentina's life span was not quite accurate, however. She did not live 15 years more after her healing. She lived 20.

* * *

Few secrets could be kept in the tight-knit society of Lequepalca. Soon the news of Valentina's healing spread all over town. People who were aware of the circumstances of her illness and who knew that no *curandero* had been able to help her, were amazed that she had recovered. Their curiosity was aroused when they learned that an evangelical stranger from Oruro wrought her healing. Many of the Colques' neighbours decided to see for themselves what manner of man was this Cirilo Lopez. Some of the first to attend the weekly Sunday meetings at Máximo Colque's house were Florencio's cousins, Froilan, Eulogio and Cresencio. Cirilo's preaching found a receptive audience in the three young men and they decided to accept the faith. But most of Lequepalca reacted negatively to the gospel that Cirilo preached. Lopez's message was one of uncompromising moral purity. A Christian, he said, must renounce alcohol and coca leaf, vices that darkened the mind and destroyed the body. As well, he must have no further dealings with the demons, since these were servants of Satan. Nor could he participate in the local dances or fiestas, because these exalted the enemies of the Lord: the world, the flesh, and the devil. These restrictions did not settle well with the *campesinos* in Lequepalca. Cirilo would not only forbid their few simple pleasures, he threatened the basic assumptions upon which their well-being depended. Angry gods were known to retaliate against communities who did not fulfil religious duties to the spirits. Natural calamity and social chaos would surely ruin Lequepalca if the community abandoned its age-old customs.

Cirilo persisted, however, in preaching holiness unto the Lord. Soon the men most concerned for the community's welfare had no choice but to confront him. One Sunday a group of village leaders showed up at the meeting in the Colque home and demanded to speak with Cirilo. The men displayed none of the customary courtesy, being heavily under the influence of *chicha*.

'Look, Lopez,' they said, 'you are going to have to change your preaching. There is no need for you to say the things you do about our customs.'

'What do you mean?' Cirilo asked. 'I am only saying what the Bible says.'

'But you are much too harsh,' they countered. They pointed to the *curandero* Quispe, one of their delegation. 'Quispe here is an evangelical like you. He has been a believer for years, but has never given us any trouble. He lets his children dance in festival processions and he himself drinks with us on occasion. He is a good *curandero*, too. He consults the spirits for healings. Why can't you be like Quispe and leave us in peace?'

Cirilo sighed and shook his head. He had very definite ideas about the kind of person a Christian should be. He could not compromise those convictions. Facing his critics, he smiled brightly. 'Jesus preached the truth, but it was not always agreeable to his listeners,' he said. 'Many of them complained, like you, that his message was too harsh. He was criticized and, in the end, crucified. But he always spoke the truth. I know I am speaking the same truth. I expect to be criticized, perhaps even killed. But I will not quit speaking the truth.'

His answer sparked an instant hostile reaction. The men all spoke at once, shouting abuse at the preacher. One husky farmer advanced upon Cirilo, fists clenched. Froilan Colque, sensing that he meant to do harm, blocked his path. His sudden movement disoriented the drunken men long enough for Florencio and Máximo to whisk Cirilo out the door and over the back wall.

'Go down to Cresencio's house, Cirilo,' the Colques urged. 'We'll meet there later.'

Meanwhile, Valentina tried to calm the intruders, who tottered about cursing Cirilo and promising what they would do to the preacher the next time they caught up with him. After a few minutes they left, uttering a final, ominous warning. 'Lopez had better ease off on the preaching or there is going to be real trouble.'

* * *

After that incident, Cirilo made less frequent visits to Lequepalca. He had two reasons for this. One, to avoid further violence, and two, because he was busy organizing a new church in Oruro. His decision to form his own congregation had been fermenting in Cirilo's mind for some time. For years he had moved in and out of various evangelical congregations. Shortly after his conversion through the ministry of the Chilean Pentecostals in Oruro, Cirilo had returned to his native Sucre. There he attended a Plymouth Brethren church and was eventually baptized by the pastor. Brethren leaders, always alert to identify and encourage promising evangelists, recognized that Cirilo had a gift for preaching. They allowed him frequent opportunities to speak in their meetings.

But after a few years in his hometown, the Bolivian Federal Petroleum Company transferred Cirilo back to Oruro. The Brethren had no congregations there and Cirilo lost contact with his mentors. He began attending one of the few evangelical churches that existed at the time. He would probably have continued attending that congregation for the rest of his life, except for two practices with which he could not agree. The first involved the question of church authority. The church was part of a denomination originally founded by missionaries from North America. Although the national church had been in existence for several decades, missionaries continued to hold decision-making power in the organization. To Cirilo, this state of affairs was intolerable. He recognized that foreigners did good work and could teach Bolivians a good deal about the Bible and theology, but he did not feel they were better equipped than his countrymen to lead. Bolivians ran their own businesses and schools and government, he reasoned, why couldn't they run their own church? Cirilo conceded that missionaries would always have a place in the church, but not necessarily at the top.

The second issue had to do with professional clergy. The Oruro congregation Cirilo attended paid its pastor a full-time salary. Cirilo's study of the New Testament, however, revealed no precedent for this kind of financial arrangement. Cirilo felt that, if a man were paid to preach, eventually he would do it for the money, not for the glory of God. Cirilo had developed a close friendship with another man in the congregation named Alberto Conde. The two men often talked about these matters. One day Cirilo made a proposal to Conde.

'Look, Alberto, we don't need to be members of this denomination any more to serve God. This church has paid preachers, which is against Bible teaching. It's dominated by foreign missionaries as well. Let's start our own church, the two of us.'

'You are fluent in Aymara and I speak Quechua,' he continued. 'We can preach to people in either language. We could hold meetings in your grocery store until we can afford to rent a hall. I would like to work in the *campo*, too. I seem to have rapport with the *campesinos*. You evangelize the city folk and I will preach to the farmers.'

Either because he shared Cirilo's convictions or because he was swayed by his friend's zeal, Alberto agreed to help start the new church. But being a bit more cautious than Cirilo, he felt it would lend legitimacy to the enterprise if they sought the endorsement of a reputable missionary.

'My cousin, Luciano Condori, has worked for years with just the right man,' Conde said. 'He is an independent missionary, not under the control of any mission board. Neither does he accept money for his work. Best of all, he has had years of experience working in Bolivia among Quechuas and Aymaras. Luciano says he understands our ways better than any foreigner he knows. His name is Homer Firestone.'

Cirilo agreed, somewhat reluctantly, to invite Dr Firestone to Oruro for a meeting. 'But let's make it clear to him that we want his help only for Bible training and counsel,' he said. 'We will do the leading.'

* * *

Angel Colque decided to be married. As custom dictated, he and his bride needed to choose godparents for the wedding. They were looking for an older couple, well-respected in the community, who could give them sound marital advice. Angel could think of no better candidates for the job than Cirilo Lopez and his wife, Francisca. Angel approached Cirilo one day at work and asked him to serve as godfather to his marriage. Cirilo agreed to accept the honour, on the condition that he be allowed to meet the bride before finally committing himself.

'I'm sure you will approve of her,' Angel assured him. 'She comes from a good family and her parents have been evangelical Christians for years.'

'What is her name?' Cirilo asked.

'Isabel Leon. She lives on Cañada Strongest Street.'

Angel arranged for Cirilo to accompany him to his fiancée's home one evening after work. They knocked on the door and were ushered into the Leon living room. Angel introduced his prospective godfather to his future in-laws, Calixto and Catalina Leon.

Cirilo, grinning broadly, looked at the couple. 'Do you remember me?' he said. 'I am Brother Cirilo.'

The Leons' puzzled expressions indicated that they did not remember him. 'Think back,' Cirilo continued. 'Years ago, when the Pentecostals came from Chile, we held meetings right here in this living room. We three became believers together, remember?'

A flicker of recognition crossed Catalina's face. 'Of course!' she exclaimed, 'Brother Cirilo!' She turned to her husband. 'This is Cirilo, from Sucre. The one who was here when you were baptized.'

At the mention of his baptism, Señor Leon recalled Cirilo, as well. He and Catalina embraced their old friend and the three of them began reminiscing about the times they had shared two decades earlier.

After a few minutes, Angel gently reminded the Leons that he had a specific purpose for this visit. 'If it be pleasing to you and to the Lord, Isabel and I would like to be married,' he said respectfully.

Calixto and Catalina already knew Angel would be asking this and had their answer prepared. They perceived that Angel was a hard worker, had a good job and would provide well for their daughter. The fact that he was a Christian believer meant that Isabel would not have to endure, as many wives did, a man given to drunkenness and womanizing. To these assets was added yet another, one that, until this moment, the Leons had not anticipated but now heartily welcomed. Cirilo Lopez would be godfather to the union. As they assented to Angel's request, the Leons tried to appear properly solemn. Cirilo offered a prayer of blessing upon the union, asking God to help the young couple build a truly Christian home. Arrangements for the ceremony were discussed over tea. Before leaving, Cirilo made a second proposal to the Leons.

'Calixto and Catalina, my heart is glad that we have met again after all these years. I believe God planned this encounter. He has called me, along with brother Alberto Conde, to raise up a new church for him here in Oruro. I believe he is calling you to help.

I want you to come this Sunday to the worship service in Brother Conde's grocery store.'

The Leons accepted his invitation and attended the gathering. A few Sundays later, at the invitation of Alberto Conde, the missionary Homer Firestone arrived in Oruro to meet with the new congregation. By then, Calixto and Catalina Leon were faithful participants in the tiny group that met to worship among the shelves in Alberto's grocery store.

* * *

The small band of evangelical believers in Lequepalca now met at Cresencio Colque's home each Sunday for worship. Life had become difficult for them. They had to hold their weekly meetings in secret, so as not to risk reprisal from their neighbours. An unofficial vigilante committee had formed to monitor the evangelicals' activities and discourage them from following their new faith. Their opponents were prepared to use force, if necessary, to keep the evangelical religion from taking hold in the Lequepalca community.

Froilan Colque found himself a special target of the vigilantes. Froilan refused to keep quiet about his faith in Jesus. He went from house to house preaching and praying for the sick. Froilan even defied Lequepalca's town fathers and preached in the main plaza of the town. He did this on 29 September, the day residents celebrated the anniversary of the founding of Lequepalca. The annual fair attracted a large crowd and Froilan chose the occasion to introduce them to the gospel. He even brought coloured posters illustrating the biblical themes he expounded. The posters attracted a large crowd as he had hoped. But in the middle of Froilan's preaching, Tito Poma abruptly interrupted the presentation and ordered the listeners to leave. To encourage them to do so, Poma ripped Froilan's Bible posters off the easel and tore them to shreds.

Froilan did not retaliate against his persecutors. Nor did he abandon his preaching. His tenacity infuriated his adversaries. They waited for another public opportunity to punish Froilan, a confrontation that would, at the same time, discredit his message. Their chance came during the inauguration ceremony for the town's new school. One of the guests of honour was Colonel Sandalio Valverde, Froilan's commanding officer in the army. Civic leaders suggested to the colonel that he invite Froilan to have a drink. The colonel called the young man to the head table.

'Colque, how are you doing?' he asked amiably.

'Very well. Thank you, Colonel,' Froilan responded.

'Here, you must have a drink with me,' Valverde said, offering Froilan a glass of *chicha*.

Froilan tried to decline as graciously as possible. 'Thank you, sir, but I do not drink.'

The colonel's expression turned suddenly stern. 'Colque, I *order* you to drink this,' he said. 'We must drink a toast to the fatherland.'

Froilan was aware that many eyes were watching him and realized that his enemies had prepared this trap in order to ruin his testimony. If he drank the *chicha* in front of the town, his neighbours would no longer lend credence to his gospel preaching. As much as Froilan loathed giving offence to the good colonel, betraying his Lord was much more loathsome to him.

'Pardon me, Colonel,' he said quietly, 'but I cannot drink it. When I was a soldier, I obeyed your orders without fail, as you well know. But now I am a civilian and you can no longer command me.'

The colonel saw that it was futile to argue with this ardent young man. 'Very well, Froilan,' he said, seeking to save them both further embarrassment, 'since you refuse my toast, I order you to wash the windows of the new school.'

Froilan's face broke into a wide grin. 'As you wish, Colonel,' he said cheerily. 'I will be only too happy to perform that order for the fatherland.'

Froilan found a pail and some rags and went to work on the school windows. His enemies, infuriated by his escape from their trap, decided to punish him for it and went to find a jug of *chicha*. Later that afternoon as Froilan was washing windows, a group of drunken men sneaked up from behind, wrestled him to the ground and pinned his arms behind his back. One man pulled on his hair and pried his chin down, forcing his mouth open. A third started pouring *chicha* down Froilan's throat. 'So you think you are too good to drink with the colonel, eh, Colque?' they taunted. Froilan gagged, the liquor burned. His assailants continued pouring until the *chicha* jug was empty.

Froilan's brother, Eulogio, discovered what was happening and ran to the school. He arrived just as Froilan's assailants were pouring out the last of the *chicha*. Eulogio shouldered his way through the mob, pulled his brother to his feet and firmly guided him to where Angel Colque was waiting in a truck. As soon as Froilan was aboard, Angel drove away. Eulogio stayed behind to hinder Froilan's persecutors from pursuing him. When these discovered Froilan had escaped, they dragged Eulogio before the town fathers and charged him with disturbing the peace. The authorities locked Eulogio in jail.

Despite insult and injury, the Colques persisted in their evangelical faith. The vigilantes persisted, as well. Froilan learned of a plot against his life and decided, for his family's sake, that he should leave Lequepalca. He hid in the hills, then made his way to La Paz. Once there, he lost himself in the anonymity of the capital, working as a stevedore in the central market.

* * *

Florencio was not living in Lequepalca during those stormy days. His job with the National Highway Service had obligated him to move to Caracollo, a town near Oruro. His enemies sent word to him there that, if he cared for his family, he had better not set foot in Lequepalca any more. From then on, Florencio made only nocturnal visits to his mother's home, arriving Saturday night after sundown and leaving Sunday before dawn.

Word of the disturbances in Lequepalca reached departmental authorities. They decided to intervene and restore order. The prefect himself came to Lequepalca to hear charges against the evangelicals and rule on the matter. The solution was simple, he said. Bolivia was officially a Roman Catholic country. Ecclesiastical law allowed, indeed it required, conscientious citizens to silence dissidents. The evangelicals would have to recant or else leave Lequepalca.

But when the prefect returned to Oruro and announced the ruling to the cabinet, it sparked immediate controversy. The sub-prefect took issue with his superior, pointing out that the national constitution guaranteed freedom of conscience. He contended that the Lequepalca evangelicals had a right to practise their religion unhindered. The sub-prefect felt so strongly about the issue that he travelled to Lequepalca personally to countermand the prefect's decree. The sub-prefect's reversal of the ruling incensed the vigilantes, who had enjoyed a short-lived victory. One thing was certain, they grumbled. Authorities or no authorities, evangelicals would continue to feel the heat.

As often happens in spiritual warfare, deliverance for the Lequepalca believers arose from another quarter. One of the most adamant enemies of the evangelicals, Antolin Vallejos, fell ill. At first, Antolin thought he could shake off the ailment with home remedies. But herbal teas and poultices failed to cure him, so Antolin consulted a *curandero*. The folk doctor followed standard procedure for diagnosing the illness. He spread an *aguayo* on the ground, placed four coins at the corners and sprinkled handfuls of coca leaves on the colourful cloth. He studied the leaves for several minutes before announcing the verdict.

'The cause of your illness is your persecution of the evangelicals,' he said gravely.

Antolin sagged in disbelief. 'There must be some mistake!'

'There is no mistake,' the *curandero* answered. 'The diagnosis surprises me as much as you, Antolin. But there can be no other explanation. You may not want to hear this, but the only way you are going to get well is to become friends with the evangelicals.'

'But, I am protecting the village from bad influences! Why should I suffer for that?'

The *curandero* assured Antolin that he had been careful in reading the signs and that they clearly pointed to the religious conflict as the cause of his disease. If he wanted to be cured, he would have to make peace with the believers. Antolin swore he would continue his campaign against the new religion, even if it killed him. It nearly did.

His condition worsened until he was too weak to get out of bed. His parents begged him to at least seek out Valentina Colque and try to make peace with her. 'She was nearly dead and was cured. Ask her to pray for you. Maybe that way you can find out what magic Cirilo Lopez used to heal her.'

'How can I ask Valentina for help?' Antolin protested. 'I have been persecuting her family. She will never help me.'

His parents went to Valentina Colque on behalf of their son. Valentina listened to their description of his illness and told them she had but one piece of advice. 'Antolin should go to Cirilo Lopez to be cured. He was the only one who was able to help me. I am sure he is the only one who can help Antolin.'

Young Vallejos detested the idea of seeking help from Cirilo, the man who had started all this trouble in the first place. But finally he admitted that the evangelist was the only man who could heal him. 'Okay, I'll go,' he said, 'but I will insist on paying him for his treatment. I will accept no charity from the man. He is capable of curing me just so he can convert me into an evangelical.'

Antolin felt utter humiliation the day he presented himself at Cirilo Lopez's door. 'But you don't have to treat me if you don't want to,' he told Cirilo.

'I will be glad to help you,' Cirilo said cheerily. 'Besides, it looks to me that, if you don't get better pretty soon, you will have to buy yourself a wooden coat.'

'A wooden coat?' Antolin asked.

'Yes, a casket,' Cirilo chuckled.

The young man was running a high fever. Cirilo immediately ordered him brought into the house and stripped of all his clothing. He explained that, to break the fever, he would wrap Antolin in sacks drenched in ice water. His relatives protested. 'You can't do that to him! He will die of pneumonia!' Cirilo pointed out that dying of pneumonia was no worse than dying of fever, and that would certainly happen if they did not obey his directions. Antolin's family conceded the point and allowed Cirilo to do what he thought best. When the sacks were ready, Cirilo laid his hands on Antolin and prayed for his recovery. He then wrapped the young man's entire body in the wet sacks 'in the name of the Father, the Son, and the Holy Spirit.' Seventy-two hours later, Antolin's fever broke. At that point, Cirilo said that he was out of danger of dying and would eventually recover from the disease. 'But you must remain in Oruro to regain your strength,' he told Antolin. 'You can stay with Florencio Colque.'

Florencio had recently moved from Caracollo to an apartment in the city and was glad to have company from Lequepalca, even a self-declared enemy. For his part, Antolin showed no sign of hostility. Florencio wondered if the three days he spent in Cirilo's house had softened his attitude toward evangelicals. The following Thursday night, Florencio invited his guest to attend Bible study with him at Alberto Conde's grocery store. Antolin would have declined, but he could think of no valid excuse. Anyway, he felt indebted to Florencio for the hospitality. At the meeting, Antolin was too ashamed to look the believers in the eye, knowing that they knew who he was and what he had been doing to their evangelical brethren in Lequepalca. But no one said anything to him about the persecution. They did, however, invite him to attend services again the following Sunday. Their cordiality caught Antolin off guard and he found himself promising to come. For the next month, Antolin did not miss a service at Alberto Conde's grocery. He typically sat with his head down, gaze fixed on the floor. He listened closely, however, to the sermons and testimonies. At the end of the month, he stood up before the little assembly and asked to speak.

'When you people came to my village and started preaching, it made me angry,' he said. 'I did not like the things that Cirilo said to us. So I persecuted you evangelicals. But tonight I have stopped being your persecutor. From now on, I am your brother.'

Shouts of 'Amen' and 'Glory to God' greeted Antolin's confession. Each person in the meeting took a turn embracing him and

welcoming him into the fellowship of believers. Some even wept,
Antolin among them.

A few days later, now completely well, he returned to his home.
Before leaving Oruro, Antolin promised Florencio and Cirilo that
he would put a stop to the pressure on their fellow believers in
Lequepalca. He kept his word. From that time on, the evangelicals
were able to worship freely with no fear of reprisal.

Froilan Colque returned home from La Paz and resumed his
efforts at spreading the gospel in Lequepalca. He found his
neighbours willing to listen to the message. In fact, many were
now embracing the new faith themselves. Among them was Tito
Poma, who came to Froilan and apologized for destroying his
Bible posters that day in the town plaza. Tito then told Froilan that
he wanted to surrender himself to God. Froilan led him in a prayer
of repentance. Getting up from his knees, Tito said that he had
something else to confess. 'Wait here,' he said, and disappeared
out the door.

Froilan did not know what Tito meant to do, but he had his
suspicions. Tito had been involved in a puzzling episode that
happened about the time Froilan learned of the threats on his life.
One of Froilan's cousins had told him the strange tale.

'One night, a band of men followed you home, Froilan,' she
said. 'They carried sticks of dynamite, planning to ambush you on
the path. Just as they were about to light the dynamite, however,
they saw a large group of people join you on the trail. They seemed
to come from nowhere. They were strangers, no one had ever seen
them in town before. They walked the rest of the way home with
you that night and the men had no chance to use the dynamite.'

'Who *were* those strangers with you? the woman asked Froilan,
when she had finished telling the story. 'None of us can figure it
out.'

Froilan recalled the night in question. He had felt a strong
premonition of danger, then it suddenly vanished. But he had
encountered no one else on the trail, either friend or foe, and
arrived home alone. 'I don't know who those people were,' Froilan
told his cousin. 'But brother Cirilo once told us about a text of

scripture, Psalm 91.11, that says, "For He will give his angels charge of you to guard you in all your ways."'

Froilan was reflecting on the intriguing experience when Tito Poma returned carrying five sticks of dynamite.

'I bought these a few months ago,' he said, showing them to Froilan. 'I swore I would use them to kill you.'

There was a long silence. Each man was thinking of the consequences, had Tito fulfilled his vow. Tito broke the silence with an earnest question. 'Tell me, Froilan, what should I do with my five sticks of dynamite? I bought them for a specific purpose, but I can't use them for that now.'

Froilan could appreciate Tito's dilemma. Vows were a measure of a man's character and were not to be taken lightly. Stories abounded in Lequepalca of demons punishing people who broke such vows. Froilan gently put his arm on Tito's shoulder and guided him to the door. 'I wouldn't worry too much about that vow if I were you, Tito,' he said. 'God has new plans for you, I'm sure he has new plans, as well, for your dynamite.'

6

Disciple

Homer Firestone lay on a narrow bench in Alberto Conde's grocery store gazing into the darkness. From the sound of their steady breathing, he knew his wife Elvira and their two teenage children, Ron and LeTaye, were already asleep on benches nearby. Homer reflected on the events of the day.

The Firestones had come from Cochabamba to meet with the group of believers that Alberto Conde and Cirilo Lopez had gathered in Oruro. Luciano Condori, the Firestones' close friend and former co-worker, had come from La Paz to introduce the family to the tiny congregation. He forewarned Homer about Cirilo's suspicion of foreign missionaries. Dr Firestone had expected a cool reception from the church and wondered if he would even be invited to speak in the meeting.

But he had underestimated the esteem the people held for Luciano Condori. They received the diminutive evangelist respectfully, delighted that a leader of his renown would visit their small congregation. They listened attentively when Luciano introduced the Firestones, nodding their appreciation when he told of their years of missionary experience in Bolivia. At Luciano's suggestion, Homer was invited to preach. When the service ended, Alberto Conde, Cirilo Lopez and Calixto Leon met with Homer and Luciano and discussed their reasons for forming the new congregation. As they explained their beliefs about how an evangelical church in Bolivia should operate, Homer sensed that he had much in common with these men.

For example, Homer strongly felt that Bolivians themselves, not foreign missionaries, should supervise business matters in the church. Although he held a PhD in anthropology and had worked for 17 years in the country, Homer knew he did not wholly understand Bolivia's social customs. Nor did he ever expect to. Despite his training and experience, Homer felt himself less qualified than the average *campesino* to make decisions for the church. 'I did not come to Bolivia to tell Bolivians what to do,' he told the three leaders. 'I think Bolivians know better than I how to do things for themselves. I will be happy to serve the church as a Bible teacher and preacher, but I will not accept any position of authority.'

Homer's attitude toward national leadership encouraged Cirilo. He decided to test the missionary's opinion on another principle. 'Brother Firestone,' he said, looking Homer intently in the eye, 'I want you to know that I will not accept – nor allow those working with me to accept – a salary for preaching the gospel.'

'It's okay with me if you don't want to be paid for doing the Lord's work,' Firestone replied. 'I'm here doing the Lord's work, too, but nobody is paying me. My wife and I make our own living.'

His answer surprised Cirilo, who smiled and thought, 'Here is a *gringo* I can work with.' Homer looked at the three Bolivian leaders and thought, 'God has surely brought us together.'

* * *

That meeting in Oruro in late 1963 would never have taken place if things had gone as planned for Homer and Elvira Firestone. Since arriving in the country in 1946, they had worked planting evangelical churches in small towns and villages throughout the departments of La Paz and Cochabamba. Elvira's training in medicine and Homer's in linguistics and anthropology well suited them for the task. The Bolivians with whom they worked respected the couple as competent professionals who understood and loved the people they served. The mission board in North America who provided their financial support regarded them as some of their finest personnel.

The Firestones worked for 17 years with the missionary board that deployed them to Bolivia. Then, quite abruptly, they decided to resign from the organization. But that decision did not mean they were terminating their ministry in Bolivia. They knew God still had much for them to do in the Andes and they intended to fulfil their calling. That conviction was severely tested. After accepting the Firestones' resignation, their former missionary board contacted the churches and individuals who supported them financially, directing that they cease all contributions to the couple. The Firestones' income from North American dried up immediately. One day a truck came and loaded up all their furniture. The family scraped enough money together to buy beds, a gas range, a table and chairs and set up house again.

Elvira owned one item of furniture with which she hoped to earn a living: a chiropractor's table. A nurse by training, Elvira had learned a bit of chiropractic technique years before, due to a headache. She suffered the headache while the family was living in Albuquerque, New Mexico, where Homer was working on his doctoral degree. Elvira took various medications, but nothing relieved the excruciating pain. Finally, she consulted a chiropractor. The doctor treated her with massage and adjustments to the spinal column. Within days, the headache disappeared. Surprised by the rapid success of the treatment, Elvira asked the doctor to teach her the basics of chiropractic therapy.

The more she learned about chiropractic medicine, the more interested she became in its practical application to her missionary work. 'I can't take pills and hypodermic needles with me everywhere I go in the *campo*,' she told her husband. 'But I always have my hands and fingers. I want to be able to use them as best I can to help alleviate suffering.' From then, Elvira began treating bad backs and muscle strains for *campesinos*, at no charge of course, on her rounds through the mountains.

When the Firestones' resignation from their sending mission forced them to begin paying their own way in Bolivia, Elvira decided to try earning money as a chiropractor. She had a hunch that city folks would benefit from massage and spinal column adjustments, and pay her for the treatment. She opened a clinic in the front room of the house. Within months, Elvira was seeing so many patients that the front room would no longer accommodate them. She had to expand the facilities. She and Homer decided to build a place of their own. They located an ideal piece of real estate, a large corner plot on a busy avenue, and bought it with their life savings. All income from Elvira's chiropractic clinic that did not go to feed and clothe the family went to buy bricks, mortar, and lumber. In the spring of 1964, Homer started construction on an A-frame building that would triple as clinic, residence and chapel.

While Elvira was launching her practice, Homer pursued his profession as a linguistic consultant. Dr Eugene Nida, President of the United Bible Society, invited him to Paraguay to evaluate a translation of the New Testament the Society was publishing in the Guaraní language. Nida was impressed with Homer's contribution to the project and the following year offered him a staff position with the Bible Society at its New York headquarters. After a year's stint at the home office, Dr Nida suggested, Homer could do field work, most likely in Africa, where the Society had a number of translation projects in progress.

It was an attractive offer. The position would give Homer an opportunity to do pioneering research in linguistic anthropology, a field of study then in its infancy. In addition to a comfortable salary package, the job offered the chance to travel the world. The only problem was, God had called Homer to Bolivia. Firestone's commitment to Andean peoples was total. Nothing, not even an invitation from one of the oldest and most respected Christian organizations in the world, could pry Homer away from his first love. So, instead of moving to New York, the Firestones stayed in Cochabamba, treating bad backs and constructing their house/chapel/clinic. On Easter Sunday, 1965, they dedicated the A-frame building, naming it *'Clínica El Libertador'* after the busy avenue on which it stood.

The Firestones had become, in modern missionary parlance, 'tentmakers'. Like the apostle Paul, who in the first Christian century supported his itinerant mission by making tents, the Firestones paid their own way to preach the gospel in a foreign land. They believed that, if God meant them to remain in Bolivia, he would supply the means. And like Paul, the Firestones would find out first hand the real meaning of 'itinerant'. Financing the construction of *El Libertador* depleted their bank account. To be able to continue living and working in Bolivia, they were going to have to earn more money, quite a bit more, in fact. To do so, they returned temporarily to the USA. Homer found a job teaching anthropology at Azusa Pacific College in California. He also pastored a small Evangelical Methodist church. Elvira assisted in the pastoral duties at the church and worked nights at a hospital. Later she took a job teaching English to immigrants. Hard work and simple living allowed them to save enough money to send Homer back to Bolivia for three visits during the next two years.

By the spring of 1967, with their two children enrolled in college, the Firestones had saved enough money to pay their passage back to Bolivia for half a year's missionary work. In January 1968, they returned north for another stint of college teaching and nursing duty, this time in Owasso, Michigan. While there, Homer completed requirements for a licence as a family therapist that permitted him to offer counselling services to clients of *Clínica El Libertador*. For the next eleven years, Homer and Elvira would lead this type of gypsy lifestyle, dividing their time between two continents. Every time they had to pack their bags and head north, they wondered when they would be coming home again to Bolivia.

But they always managed to come home again. And each time they did, they found the church Cirilo Lopez and Alberto Conde had planted in Oruro growing like wildfire.

* * *

Homer Firestone was one reason why the church in Bolivia expanded rapidly, both for what he did for the believers and for what he did not do for them. What he did was to encourage evangelists to concentrate their efforts on *campesinos*, instead of trying to convert city folks with whom they had little in common.

He also gave them a biblical foundation for their work, conducting short, intensive Bible courses to train preachers. What Homer did not do was to evangelize the *campesinos* himself. He accompanied bands of evangelists to rural campaigns, but always as the coach, never as the star, of the team. In public meetings, he stayed in the background as much as he could.

Homer had specific motives for keeping a low profile. For one, he felt that native speakers of Aymara and Quechua were better qualified to preach to *campesinos* than he was. Other missionaries took issue with him at this point, insisting that he as an effective communicator should speak the native dialect. 'Of course it's important to know enough of the language to converse on an informal basis and to understand what is being said in meetings,' he responded. 'But why should I subject them to my poor stammering in the pulpit? Bolivian preachers are much better at communicating the message to their countrymen than I will ever be.' Homer the anthropologist had learned that people better identify with communicators from their own culture. They will listen politely to a foreign preacher, but fail to grasp what the sermon has to say to them personally. But when they hear the same message from a man who looks like them, talks like them, and lives like them, they realize how much sense it makes.

Another reason why Homer maintained a low profile was because he noted how the humble *campesinos* treated him when he arrived in a rural village: like a king. Homer always slept in the best bed, ate the best food and was invited to preach at every service. He declined the latter honour whenever he could in order not to overshadow Bolivian colleagues. When the believers insisted that Dr Firestone preach, he always did so in Spanish, depending upon a native speaker to interpret the message. 'One way to avoid making national leaders dependent on the foreign missionary,' he once explained to a friend, 'is for the missionary to maintain his dependence on national leaders.'

Perhaps the most significant contribution Homer made to the cause of the new church was his reputation. In a country where the majority of the population has no formal education, academic titles command great respect. Those who have them, no matter how inconsequential the rank, enjoy esteem. Those who do not, however capable the person, are disregarded. This proved to be an obstacle for the humble believers of the Oruro church. Few had ever seen the inside of a classroom, none had studied the Bible in an academic institution. When they began to expound scriptural truth, preachers from other evangelical churches dismissed them as incompetent.

'What makes you people think you can preach?' the detractors asked. 'Who of you has studied in a Bible institute or seminary?'

'It's true that we have not studied in an institution,' the believers admitted, 'but we are learning from our missionary, Dr Homer Firestone. He is a college professor. By the way, does your missionary have PhD? Are any of your co-workers college lecturers?' The critics fell silent. The believers preached on.

Cirilo Lopez was another reason why the church grew. Cirilo possessed genuine charisma. When he preached at open air campaigns in his strong baritone voice, people were drawn to him. His charisma was not merely a natural gift, but the result of a disciplined lifestyle focussed on God. He had spent so much time reading his Bible that he could quote much of it by heart. Froilan Colque was particularly impressed with Cirilo's command of Scripture. 'Pastors from other churches, men who had studied in the Bible institutes, came to debate with Cirilo,' Froilan recalled. 'He flattened all their arguments. They would object to a point of doctrine and he would say, "But what does it say in chapter such and such, verse such and such?" They could not answer him.'

Believers in the Oruro congregation once asked Cirilo to teach them how to study the Scriptures. 'You want Bible studies?' Cirilo replied. 'Okay, we will conduct Bible studies. On the top of a mountain. Before dawn. While we fast and pray.' Thereafter, every third month, on the first Sunday of the month and in the wee hours of the morning, Cirilo led his flock to the crest of a small peak outside Oruro. There they separated from each other a stone's throw, just as Jesus and his disciples had done in Gethsemane. Each believer knelt with an open Bible before him and prayed for God to teach him what he needed to know. It was a crude method of theological study rarely pursued since the days of Jesus and his disciples.

Rigorous discipline is beneficial in forming Christian character, but following Jesus involves joy and celebration as much as self-denial. Cirilo encouraged believers to enjoy their faith. Once a congregation was established, he taught them to celebrate a *junta* once a year. In Spanish *'junta'* literally means 'bring together'. Cirilo added another definition, 'spiritual fiesta', and urged rural congregations to invite neighbouring villages to these weekend celebrations. The *junta* typically began on Friday or Saturday afternoon, sometimes with a wedding. At night, after an hours-long preaching service, visiting musical bands presented special music for the enjoyment of anyone who cared to listen. The collective concert sometimes lasted into the early hours of the morning. The audience joined in singing familiar hymns and learned new ones. Two services on Sunday, one at dawn and another at mid-morning, were followed by feasting. The host church 'killed the fatted calf' in order to serve the best to their guests. The meeting closed with a baptismal ceremony, provided the *junta* site was close to a stream large enough to immerse new converts.

Florencio Colque was another reason why the church in Oruro grew. Following the example set by Homer and Cirilo, he dedicated most of his non-working hours to the Lord. The challenge of announcing the gospel in places where Christ had not yet been preached motivated him, as it motivated Cirilo, Homer and other evangelists.

The young man's decision to devote himself to preaching was, you might say, accidental. Football had been his first love since childhood. Cirilo did not share Florencio's enthusiasm for the sport, however. He did not hesitate to tell his young friend what he thought about football. Like most of his opinions, Cirilo justified this one with a reference to scripture.

'According to 1 Corinthians 6.19, your body is the temple of the Holy Spirit,' Cirilo told Florencio. 'You have a responsibility before God to take care of his temple. Now, let's say you go out and play football and break a leg. That wouldn't be taking care of God's temple, now would it?'

Florencio always followed Cirilo's advice, except when it came to football. Florencio had developed a reputation for his play. He could not simply walk away from the game. Besides, how could he explain to his friends that God disliked sports? Then it happened. Florencio broke his leg playing football. Not just broke, smashed. The injury put him in a hip-to-toe cast for several months. They were months of discomfort, boredom and worst of all, worry. Because he was unable to work, Florencio feared he might lose his job with the National Highway Service. He was at home, deeply depressed, when Cirilo came to visit him. Florencio expected sympathy from his mentor. He got none.

'Florencio, you cannot take God lightly,' Cirilo said. 'He will not be mocked. Whatever a man sows, he will also reap.'

Florencio hung his head while Cirilo continued the lecture. 'Do you know why this happened to you? Because you still have doubts about following the Lord. You say with your lips that you believe, but your heart is far from God. He is testing you, Florencio, to see if you will trust Him with your whole heart.'

After Cirilo's visit, Florencio thought long and hard about his admonition. Finally, he had to admit the man was right. From somewhere inside him (yet not inside) a voice called. God was inviting him, compelling him, to draw closer. A part of Florencio deeply desired to answer the call, but another part resisted. What would God ask him to do? Florencio was not at all sure what the future would bring if he were to 'sell out' to God. But the call was compelling and, in the end, he surrendered to it. When he did, he no longer felt depressed. He still wore the cast on his leg. His injury still irritated him and his future remained uncertain. But somehow those things did not bother him any more. In fact, they could not bother him anymore. His mind was set on other things.

Florencio began reading the New Testament with avid interest. In six months, he read through the four Gospels. They were the first books in his life that Florencio read in their entirety. The project produced two results: a marked improvement in his reading ability and a profound change in his understanding of Jesus. The more he pondered Jesus' message, the less he thought about football. Eventually, the sport ceased to interest him.

Cirilo understood what was happening to Florencio. One day, toward the end of the young man's convalescence, he remarked, 'Florencio, God has allowed this accident to happen to you to prepare you. He has given you the opportunity to study the Bible these past months because he has work for you to do. Will you do it?'

Florencio had his answer ready. 'I will.' He meant exactly what he said.

* * *

The work Cirilo spoke of was no armchair job. The rapid growth of the church required its ministers to travel constantly to keep up with the expansion. So many invitations to preach in rural villages came to Cirilo that he could not accept them all. In those cases, he chose an apprentice preacher to go in his stead. Soon after the doctor removed Florencio's cast, Cirilo sent him on his first preaching mission. The young man left Oruro Saturday evening on his bicycle to visit the church in Tiraque, 37 kilometres distant.

'You get there by heading out to Pasto Grande and turning west,' Cirilo instructed. 'If you get lost, ask directions from the local people. When you get to Tiraque, ask for Brother Flores. He will give you lodging for the night.'

With this orientation Florencio left town with his Bible, his bedroll and his bicycle. It soon grew dark and began to rain, then to sleet, then to hail. The bike was impossible to pedal in the mud so Florencio carried it. The thought of turning back to spend the night in Oruro never occurred to him. After a few hours, the weather and fatigue drove him to seek shelter. He heard a dog bark in the darkness and followed the sound to a farmhouse. The owner answered his knock, listened to his plea, but said it would be impossible for him the sleep there because the house was already full. Florencio trudged on. Before he could reach the next farm house, the owner heard him coming and shouted, 'Who is that going there in the dark? Only thieves go around at night!' Florencio thought it prudent not to ask for lodging in that place.

When he identified himself as an evangelist at a third farmhouse, he was relieved to learn this was a family of evangelical believers. The head of the house, however, was reluctant to admit a stranger into his home, even one who claimed to be a brother in Christ. The man questioned Florencio about his doctrinal beliefs while the young fellow stood in the cold rain, teeth chattering uncontrollably. At last he said, 'We are sorry that we can't let you stay with us for the night, but you are not far from Brother Flores' house. Just follow this path and you will find it on your left.'

Sure enough, Florencio found the house down the road on his left and discovered that Brother Flores had gone away on a trip. His nephew, who had never heard of Florencio Colque, hesitated to let him in. Florencio stood shivering on the stoop while the young man conducted another interrogation. After satisfying himself that Florencio was indeed a commissioned preacher from the church in Oruro, the nephew invited him to step inside. That night, Florencio slept like a log. The next morning he preached to a tiny group of believers assembled in Brother Flores' patio and prayed for the sick.

On another occasion, Florencio was invited to preach at the *junta* in Collpa, a small place high in the mountain range on the border separating the departments of Oruro and Cochabamba. Collpa lay one hour's walk from the nearest road. Florencio was unable to get a truck out of Oruro until late in the evening, but he did not worry about getting lost. He had been in Collpa once before and was certain he could remember the way. He reached the area at about 10 p.m., stepped off the truck and paid his fare. He waited a few minutes after the vehicle lumbered off so that his eyes could adjust to the darkness. The night was moonless but he could distinguish the outline of the massive peaks by the light of the stars. He started off at a brisk pace through the canyon he knew must lead to Collpa. He hoped to reach the *junta* in time to deliver a brief message before the worshippers launched their night-long vigil of singing.

He did not make it. In the darkness, Florencio had confused the landmarks and chosen the wrong canyon. An hour and a half into his hike, a faint suspicion came upon him that he was lost. After two hours, his knew he must be. He had no idea where he was or where Collpa lay. There was nothing to do except hole up for the night and wait for morning. This plan presented some risk. The night air at 4,000 metres' altitude is thin and bitterly cold, especially in winter. Happily, Florencio knew what to do to keep from freezing to death. He cut clumps of dry bunchgrass and improvised a nest for himself. Settling into the pile of straw, he pulled his woollen poncho about his ears and fell asleep.

At the first light of dawn, he awoke. He studied the surrounding peaks to calculate his position and headed in the direction of Collpa. This time he was lucky. Florencio walked into the *junta* just as the believers were serving breakfast. They asked him why he was so late arriving. As he narrated his adventure, the locals became greatly amused. 'Imagine, a grown man getting lost in these parts!' they sniggered. 'Why, our toddlers can find their way around here with their eyes closed!'

No one seemed concerned that Florencio had had to sleep in the open air in sub-freezing temperatures. Nor did he himself grumble about risking his life to preach at the Collpa *junta*. After all, a soldier of the cross was expected to take such trials in his stride. Nevertheless, the next time the Collpa believers invited Florencio to preach, he was careful to arrive before sundown.

* * *

Florencio and his fellow evangelists endured harsh weather and exhausting travel for two reasons. First because, to their way of thinking, these were small inconveniences compared to what Jesus endured during his earthly sojourn. Second because they witnessed startling transformations in the lives of people who heeded the call to repentance. Casiano Condori was a typical example. Casiano and his wife, Florencia, lived in Calapata, near Lequepalca. The Calapata valley had good soil and a river that supplied year-round irrigation. The Condori family was prospering, thanks to their fine crops of carrots, onions and barley. Casiano owned more than two hundred sheep and five yoke of oxen and had begun to save for the purchase of a flatbed truck. He planned to use the truck to carry his fine harvests to market in Oruro.

The Calapata community regarded Casiano as a gifted leader. The local priest was training him as a catechist and promised to send him to Panama to study theology. *Curanderos* tried to persuade him to take up their craft, as well. 'With your abilities you could make a lot of money,' they assured him.

But then Casiano's world came apart. Florencia fell ill with a debilitating disease. Her skin turned a leprous white. She had no strength to get out of bed, much less to do any work. Casiano had to take over the household duties and care for their two sons. He took his wife to every *curandero* he knew for miles around, but she did not improve. Casiano then resorted to doctors and hospitals in the city, again to no avail. To pay the medical fees and to buy the herbs and medicines the folks healers prescribed, Casiano had to sell first his sheep, then his oxen.

As Florencia's illness worsened, she began to hallucinate. She saw serpents crawling on the ceiling and falling into her bed. Casiano worried that she would harm herself in her delirium, so he stayed awake at night to calm her when she awoke screaming. He started drinking heavily to escape the pressure and worry. Steadily Casiano turned into an alcoholic. He also began chewing coca to stay awake at night at Florencia's bedside. He soon became addicted to the leaf. He developed a tolerance to the narcotic, so that even large doses failed to keep him alert. He took to wearing a garland of thorns around his neck, so that when he dozed and his head nodded, the pricks would startle him back to wakefulness.

Casiano's alcohol and coca habits were expensive. The vices, along with Florencia's medical costs, gradually reduced him to a pauper. His flock of sheep dwindled from 200 to just 30 animals. Of his five yoke of sturdy oxen, only a cow and her calf remained. Because he had little time to spend in the fields, Casiano's crops were but a fraction of those he had harvested in former years. For three years Florencia was confined to her bed. When the Condori family's fortunes were at their lowest ebb, Florencia's eldest brother died. Everyone assumed, though no one said so, that Florencia would soon follow him.

All Saints' Day arrived that year and the family had to provide the customary gifts for the grave of Florencia's brother, Geronimo Ramos. Casiano went to his surviving brother-in-law, Julian, to inquire what arrangements he was making.

'I'm not preparing anything at all,' Julian Ramos responded. 'Since becoming an evangelical, I don't believe in such superstition anymore.'

Casiano could not believe what he was hearing. Julian was placing himself in a dangerous position. Those who did not visit their close relatives' graves on All Saints' suffered retribution from the devil. Geronimo's was an especially risky case because of the circumstances of his death. He had not passed away peacefully. A 17-year-old girl had strangled him with a slingshot, later claiming that Geronimo had tried to rape her while she was alone pasturing her sheep. Since Geronimo had died violently, his ghost would be on the prowl for vengeance. It would certainly do harm to anyone who failed to show proper respect, even his brother Julian. Casiano concluded that if his brother-in-law's new religion gave him the confidence to challenge the wrath of a vengeful spirit cheated of its gifts on All Saints' Day, this faith must be powerful indeed. Casiano decided to investigate this evangelical phenomenon at the next *junta* celebrated within walking distance of his home.

He had not long to wait. The church in Chicuela Alta scheduled its annual *junta* for the weekend following All Saints'. Casiano set out on Saturday afternoon to see for himself what gave these evangelicals such fearless faith. He did not want to get too close, however, so he stood behind a boulder and studied the proceedings from a distance. He listened to their singing, watched as they knelt to pray and caught snatches of the sermon. He could distinguish nothing unusual about the worship and was at a loss to explain how Julian could have been duped into joining this meek, little band.

After the service concluded, the worshippers lined up and their hosts served supper. Casiano now guessed the source of the believers' magic. Most likely, a secret ingredient in the food produced their faith. He watched intently as they ate to see what effect the meal would have on them. Alvina de Torrez, an aged widow in charge of the cooking, happened to look in his direction and spotted Casiano. Alvina made her way to where he was hiding before Casiano, engrossed as he was in observing the diners, saw her coming.

'Good afternoon, Casiano,' she greeted cheerily. 'Won't you serve yourself a plate of food?'

This was an offer that he would not, under any circumstance, accept.

'Thank you, I've already eaten,' he lied.

'Here then,' Alvina offered, 'take this plate to your wife.'

'She can't eat it, she's sick.'

'Well then, take it for your two boys. I'm sure they would like something to eat.' The woman would not be put off.

'But I have nothing to carry it in.'

'That's okay, take the plate.'

'But it might break on the way.'

'Here then,' Alvina said, producing a cloth napkin and emptying the plate into it, 'carry the food in this. And you needn't worry about getting it back to me.'

Casiano could think of no more excuses, so he accepted the food. He was sure it contained a powerful herb that would cast a spell over anyone who ate it and turn them into an evangelical. He wanted to dump it out on the way home but something restrained him. Upon his arrival, Florencia and the boys asked what he had in the bundle. They were delighted to find out it was supper, for they had had none and it was late. Reluctantly, Casiano gave them the food. 'But I'll not touch it,' he told them sternly. 'I'm not going to be infected by those evangelicals.' Instead, he stuffed a wad of coca leaves into his mouth to dull his hunger pangs and sat down to observe what effect the food would have on his wife and sons.

Nothing out of the ordinary happened to them, either that night or the next day. Impressed by the kindness of Alvina de

Torrez, Florencia made a suggestion to her husband. Why not bring an evangelical to the house to pray for her?

Surprisingly, Casiano assented. He had concluded that the believers' magic posed no threat to him after all. He went to see his brother-in-law, Julian Ramos. 'I want you to bring one of those brothers to the house to pray for Florencia,' he told Julian. 'Make sure it's one of those who knows how to tap her on the head with the big black book. But just one, you understand, no more. I'll be watching for you and if you have two or three with you, I'll not let you in.'

The next day, Julian brought Froilan Colque to the Condoris' house. Casiano led them to his wife's bedside, then excused himself and retreated to the patio to chew coca. Froilan talked with the sick woman, asking questions about her ailment. At length he inquired if she had the faith to believe that God could make her well. She replied by saying that she expected Froilan to make her well.

'I can pray for you,' he explained, 'but only God can heal you. And you should know that he will do so only if he chooses.'

Florencia wanted to know if there was anything she could do to improve her chances. Froilan replied that she could surrender herself to God. 'I don't guarantee that he will heal you even then. But if he doesn't, and you die, at least you will be prepared to meet him face to face.'

This made sense to Florencia. She explained to Froilan that she had reached the point in her suffering where she no longer dreaded dying. At times, in fact, she thought it must be better than living, given her present circumstances. She acknowledged the wisdom of preparing her soul, just in case she had to face God sometime in the near future.

'And what about your husband, Casiano?' Froilan asked. 'I think it would be best if he joined you in this decision.'

They called Casiano in from the patio and informed of his wife's decision to receive Christ. Froilan stated that, in his opinion, a wife should not take this important step unless her husband agree to join her. Casiano objected, saying that it was all right with him if his wife wanted this new religion but that he was satisfied to remain as he was. Froilan continued to insist. It appeared to Florencia that he was not going to permit her to accept Christ unless her husband did, as well. She pleaded with Casiano to convert. Finally he yielded.

'All right, I'll do this for Florencia's sake. Then no one can say I didn't do everything possible to make her well.'

The couple knelt before Froilan and repeated a prayer. Afterward, Froilan prayed alone, asking God to deliver the Condoris from sin and give them eternal life. Then he prayed for Florencia, that she would be restored to full health.

Something happened to Casiano Condori during those prayers. When he got up from his knees, he spat out the wad of coca leaves he had been chewing. The two pounds of leaf stored in the closet he took out to the patio and burned. Next he gathered up all the bottles of alcohol in the house, carried them to a dry streambed, and emptied them into the sand. Something, or Someone, was telling him to get rid of these unhealthy habits. From that day on, he tasted neither alcohol nor coca ever again.

When Casiano had finished detoxifying the house, Froilan made a frightening proposal. Casiano and Florencia ought to be baptized, he said, at the next *junta* in Lequepalca. This frightened Casiano because he was convinced that immersion in the river would kill his wife.

'Moisture makes her skin swell,' he explained to Froilan. 'When a drop of water hits her hand, it brings up a blister. We don't touch the blisters for fear they will burst.' Casiano could envision his wife emerging from the baptismal pool horribly bloated and about to explode.

But Florencia was willing. 'If I die, well, it can't be so bad as what I'm going through now,' she said.

So on Easter Sunday morning, Casiano and Florencia Condori were among the new believers lined up at the river in Lequepalca to undergo baptism. Casiano fully expected this day to be his wife's last. He dreaded what would happen to her when she entered the river and watched, petrified with fear, as Cirilo Lopez immersed Florencia in the water. But then the unexpected happened. Florencia stepped out on the riverbank and Casiano saw that her skin, instead of swelling up, was beginning to regain its natural colour. Casiano touched her. To his astonishment, the flesh was soft and warm. Could it be?

It was. In a few days, Florencia was back doing her household chores. She regained the weight she had lost and never again experienced hallucinations or the other symptoms of the strange disease. Some months later, an event occurred that once and for all confirmed her healing. Florencia had a baby.

The Condori home returned to the tranquil rhythm it had not known for more than three years. Casiano and his two sons laboured in the fields, cultivating their crops of onions, barley and carrots and rebuilding their herd of livestock. It took some years for them to regain their lost prosperity. But in time, their flock of sheep numbered more than 200 animals once again. In time, Casiano ploughed his fields with yoke of sturdy oxen once again. And in time, he was able to buy that flatbed truck to carry his abundant harvests to market in Oruro.

* * *

Flatbed trucks are the backbone of Bolivia's rural transportation system. They vastly outnumber cars and busses on back roads in the mountains, carrying passengers and produce to market and home again. The practical advantages over other types of vehicles include the trucks' ability to traverse rocky roads and swollen rivers and to carry anything the rural traveller wants to transport. This may include kids, pigs, sheep, llamas, potato crops, or all of the above.

Cirilo Lopez had decided he needed a flatbed truck. He saw the potential a vehicle would have for evangelistic work and encouraged Angel Colque to buy one. The young man scraped enough money together to buy a used Toyota, well past its prime. The vintage truck required a special chauffeur, one who could not only drive it but also fix it when it broke down on back roads in the mountains, which happened with regularity. Florencio Colque had gained experience in both tasks while working for the National Highway Service, so Angel asked him to drive the truck.

Angel also acquired an accordion, which he learned to play by ear. When he played it in the evangelistic campaigns, people gathered to hear the new and curious music. With Angel on the accordion and Florencio at the wheel, Cirilo found himself preaching to ever larger crowds in villages farther and farther from Oruro. *Juntas* were becoming very popular in these villages. The first one Cirilo and Homer Firestone conducted in Pasto Grande attracted 200 people. Its success inspired the Colque clan to sponsor a similar meeting in Lequepalca.

Florencio, Froilan, Cresencio and Eulogio decided to build a chapel on Colque family land to accommodate the visitors they expected for the *junta*. With help from Antolín Vallejos, Tito Poma and other believers in Lequepalca, the adobe church was finished by Easter 1966, the date they chose for the annual *junta*. To the young men's dismay, however, their new church proved grossly inadequate. Nearly 500 people showed up to celebrate the Easter *junta*, so most of the crowd could not even fit inside. Failure to properly accommodate their guests propelled the Lequepalca believers to immediately begin construction on a larger building next door. The Colques and their neighbours calculated that the second tabernacle would hold 500 worshippers, and indeed the entire *junta* crowd was able to squeeze into it the following year. However, 370 new believers were baptized on that second Easter Sunday at Lequepalca. This cast serious doubt on the new tabernacle's future usefulness.

Sure enough, so many people came to Lequepalca in 1968 that the 500-capacity tabernacle proved woefully insufficient. *Junta* organizers had no choice but to hold the meetings outside in the open air. Evidently, no one seemed to mind the inconvenience. In following years the Lequepalca *junta* continued to grow until Homer Firestone and Cirilo Lopez were preaching to crowds of 3,000 and 5,000 each Easter weekend.

The original chapel in Lequepalca was used at the Easter *juntas* to celebrate weddings and pray for the sick. Not everyone who wanted to use the tiny building could do so at once. On Saturday, brides and grooms queued up outside the front door to wait their turn to be joined in wedlock. At the back door, where the sick entered seeking prayer, a deacon was stationed to admit them one at a time, so as to conserve enough room for them to kneel inside the building. The big tabernacle was turned into sleeping quarters for the women and children. Most of the crowd could not fit in, of course. These folks slept outdoors in brush arbours, makeshift tents or in the flatbed trucks that brought them to the *junta*.

7

Husband and Father

Julia Leon, youngest daughter of Calixto and Catalina Leon, had just completed her eighteenth year when Cirilo Lopez paid a visit to the Leon home. He explained that he had an important matter to talk over with Julia. The rest of the family excused themselves and left Cirilo and Julia alone. Cirilo came right to the point.

'I come on behalf of Florencio Colque,' he began. 'He is thinking about getting married and, of all the young women in the church, has cast his eye on you, Julia.' He paused to see what reaction this news would cause.

Julia looked steadily at Cirilo. Her brown eyes betrayed no flicker of emotion.

Cirilo said, 'Would you like to marry Florencio?'

'No.'

'Why not?' Cirilo asked, surprised.

'Because I am not in love with him.'

Cirilo shifted in his chair. He had not expected such a blunt refusal. When Florencio had asked him to talk with Julia about the prospect of matrimony, the young man seemed confident that she would accept his proposal. Cirilo assumed that Julia had expressed her affection to Florencio. Evidently that was not the case. Cirilo could see definite advantages to the union, however.

'Are you in love with another young man?' he asked.

'No.'

Cirilo relaxed a bit. 'Well then, I don't see why you can't consider marrying Florencio. He's a good man, a believer. What's more, all of his family are believers.'

Julia reminded Cirilo of a fact he seemed to have overlooked. 'He is so much older than I,' she said. 'Why, he must be at least 26 or 27!'

Cirilo smiled. 'I see what you mean, Julia. But I don't think that is a big problem. The difference seems great now, but as you both grow older the gap will narrow. Personally, I don't think you can find a better husband than Florencio, no matter what his age.'

Julia was not sure. Like all the young people in the church, she respected Cirilo's judgement. Still, when it came to a decision that would affect the rest of her life, she hesitated. Cirilo did not want to pressure the young girl into a marriage against her will. He proposed a course he hoped would remove her doubts.

'This is what we will do,' he said. 'You and Florencio will inform the church, by letter, that you are contemplating marriage. You will ask them to fast and pray for you. For three months, you and Florencio will seek God's will in the matter. If, at the end of the three months, either one of you is unsure about marrying, then you will be under no obligation to do so.'

This seemed a sensible course to Julia and she agreed. For the next three months, she and Florencio meditated on the prospect of marrying each other, assessing the comparative advantages of the union. Above all, the two sought to know the will of God in the matter. Julia, in particular, observed Florencio's attitude toward her during that time, to see if she could detect a change. If he were inclined to treat her with too much familiarity, as though she were already his fiancée, it would mean that he was not taking their covenant seriously. She would not commit herself to a man who failed to treat such an important matter with sincerity. But Florencio did not disappoint. During the trial period, he displayed the same gentlemanly respect toward Julia that he had always shown. She decided she could trust him. Her regard for Florencio deepened. She eventually realized that he was, as Cirilo said, the type of man she wanted for a husband. At the end of the three months, the two decided to be married.

They went to Cirilo to inform him of their decision. He was delighted and arranged for the civil ceremony immediately. 'It is not a good testimony for believers to live together in concubinage,' he explained. Florencio and Julia had expected Cirilo to insist that they be legally married before living together. Though trial marriages of a year or more were still common practice in the *campo*, believers living in the city were expected to set an enlightened example. After agreeing on the date and time for the civil ceremony, Florencio asked Cirilo to do them the honour of serving as godfather to their marriage.

Cirilo sighed and looked at his young friends with a sad smile. 'As much as I would like to, I cannot be your godfather,' he said.

'Why not?' the couple asked, simultaneously.

'Because I am not a good godfather,' Cirilo replied. 'I don't understand why, but I seem to spoil my godchildren. They all are faithful believers when they marry. But then it seems that every one goes the way of the world.'

Florencio and Julia knew he was referring, among others, to Angel and Isabel. In the early years of their marriage, Florencio's stepbrother and Julia's sister had been strong in their faith. But lately, Angel was using his flatbed truck less on Sundays for the Lord's work and more for personal business. The allure of materialism seemed to have seduced him. He and Isabel were often absent from church services. Florencio could not understand why Cirilo blamed himself for his godchildren's lapses, but neither could he convince his mentor to serve as godfather to the marriage. Cirilo ended the interview by promising to secure a suitable substitute.

'Don't worry,' he reassured the young couple, 'I'll see to it that you have the best godparents in Oruro.'

A few days later, Florencio and Julia repeated their vows before the Justice of the Peace, becoming husband and wife by law. Having completed this legal requirement, they could then celebrate their marriage with a church wedding. They intended to do so before long. Meanwhile, Florencio and Julia would live together with her parents, Calixto and Catalina Leon.

Circumstances beyond their control delayed their church wedding, however. Two years passed before Alberto Conde married them in the storefront chapel in Oruro. By that time their first son, José, was ten months old.

* * *

The wedding of Florencio Colque and Julia Leon was one of the last celebrations held in the church that Alberto Conde and Cirilo Lopez pastored jointly. A few months afterward, the two leaders divided the congregation. As with most church splits, the reasons for the division were trivial. The evangelical churches in Oruro had decided to cooperate in an inter-denominational programme called 'Evangelism in Depth'. The North American missionaries who conceived and directed the project, had set an ambitious goal: to visit every home in the city with literature explaining the salient points of the gospel. Alberto Conde believed that his congregation should be involved in the ecumenical campaign. One Sunday he announced the plan in church and encouraged members to sign up as volunteers to canvass the neighbourhood.

Cirilo happened to be visiting a *junta* in the countryside on that Sunday. When he returned to Oruro and heard people talking about Evangelism in Depth, he demanded to know what was happening. The plan did not please him at all. The following week, he stood up in the church meeting and strongly urged the members not to cooperate in the campaign.

Cirilo's opposition to the inter-denominational project was based on the same reasoning that originally led him to form the church with Alberto Conde. 'This programme is dominated by foreigners, who have foreign ways of doing things,' he argued. 'We left their churches to go our own way. How can we go back to them now?'

Cirilo's opposition to Evangelism in Depth sparked a heated debate. It was clear that he and Alberto stood on opposite sides of the issue. Alberto had publicly promoted the campaign and felt he would lose face in Oruro's evangelical community if he reneged on his promise to participate in Evangelism in Depth. When it became clear that Cirilo would not join him, Alberto drew the line.

'Every one who sees eye to eye with me is welcome to stay here in this room,' he said. 'Those who disagree may show themselves out the door.'

Cirilo walked out of the meeting, followed by a sizeable group of believers. From then on, he met with his flock in Calixto Leon's parlour. Alberto continued preaching to those who attended services at his grocery store.

The schism between Cirilo Lopez and Alberto Conde puzzled the believers. Many never understood how or why it happened. Some said that Alberto had become jealous of Cirilo's popularity and was seeking a pretext to push him out of leadership. Others speculated that Cirilo, who depended on Alberto's ability to speak Aymara, no longer needed his support once he himself became fluent in the language. But the questions were never answered because neither of the two men ever spoke to their respective congregations about the matter. To each other, they did not speak at all.

The church split created a problem for Homer Firestone. He had promised to help both Cirilo and Alberto build up the national church. But that was no longer possible. If he helped one leader, the other would rebuff him. If he withdrew his support from both, he suspected their congregations would succumb to continual squabbling, more intent on outdoing one another than on carrying on the Lord's work. Homer the anthropologist realized that the differences between Cirilo and Alberto were cultural more than theological. Alberto Conde, born and raised in La Paz, followed urban values. He was class-conscious, upwardly mobile and concerned that the church be respectable. Cirilo Lopez was a simpler man, a down-to-earth *campesino*. He wanted the church to be practical. When it came to evangelistic strategy, Dr Firestone sensed he had more in common with Cirilo than Alberto.

For months, the two groups had no contact with one another. Florencio and Julia Colque, who continued to worship and work with Cirilo, often saw Alberto Conde on the street, but he never greeted them. Nor did Alberto attend *juntas* anymore. Advent rolled around that year. According to custom, the believers gathered at Calixto Leon's home for the Christmas Eve service. But that evening, Cirilo said that he could not truly celebrate the spirit of the season while he still harboured animosity toward Alberto Conde. He proposed that, instead of meeting in the Leons' parlour, they should all go over to Alberto's store and set things right.

If Alberto Conde was pleased to see Cirilo and his cortège when they trooped into his storefront that evening, he did not show it. The service went on as usual. Alberto gave the sermon. During the customary time for greetings, Cirilo stood up to speak. He began by recalling happier days when all present had worshipped together in harmony and lamented the fact that they were now divided. He acknowledged his responsibility in causing the schism and asked for pardon from those he had offended.

When he had ended his apology, he walked up tohe Alberto Conde and stuck out his hand. 'I especially want to ask you to forgive me, Brother Alberto,' he said.

Alberto replied, 'I forgive you, Brother Cirilo.' He gripped Cirilo's hand and the two men embraced.

From then on, Alberto and Cirilo were friends again. They greeted each other on the street, visited each other's home and prayed for one another. But never again did they work together in the church. They could shake hands as friends, but they would not join hands as partners.

* * *

In spite of her loyalty to Cirilo Lopez, Catalina Leon signed up to help with the Evangelism in Depth campaign. Like the other volunteers, she attended weekly classes to learn how to canvass her neighbourhood and talk with strangers about Jesus Christ. Though her inability to speak Spanish handicapped her somewhat, Catalina soon mastered the training and was on the street, knocking on doors.

Cirilo remained sceptical of this evangelistic method, but Catalina's zeal impressed him. It amazed Cirilo that the Leons, a rather reserved family, had produced an extroverted soul-winner like Catalina. 'I don't think you are Catalina's real daughter,' he chided Julia. 'Your mother is such a firebrand but you are quiet as a mouse!' Julia blushed.

One day Catalina was taking sun on the sidewalk in front of her home when a woman approached her. 'Excuse me,' the stranger said shyly, 'but I wonder if you could tell me which of these houses belong to the gypsies.'

'Gypsies?' Catalina asked, puzzled. 'There are no gypsies on this street.'

'But, they told me a group of young gypsy women lived together in a house on Cañada Strongest Street,' the woman insisted, nervously. 'Please, you must tell me where they are.'

It suddenly occurred to Catalina the reason why the woman was looking for gypsies on her street. Doña Consuelo's brothel operated two doors down from the Leons' house. The prostitutes, all strangers to the community, kept to themselves and never stayed long in town. It was understandable that a rumour was circulating that they were gypsies.

'The young women you are looking for are not gypsies. They are, ah, another sort,' Catalina said delicately. 'Tell me, though, why are you looking for gypsies?'

The stranger looked up and down the street to make sure no one could overhear their conversation. 'I need their magic,' she said quietly.

With some hesitation the woman explained her dilemma. Her name was Paulina Centeno, she said, and she lived in Sorocachi. Until recently, everything had gone well with her family. Then her eldest daughter suddenly died. Soon afterward, her second daughter passed away. The tragedies could not be attributed to mere natural causes. Neighbours told the Centenos that they had been bewitched, that an enemy had cast a spell on their three daughters. Only one of the girls remained alive and Paulina was desperate to protect her from death.

Catalina listened sympathetically to Señora Centeno's story. When she had finished, Catalina said, 'I don't think the gypsies could help you, even if you did find them. Why don't you try the church instead? A group of believers meets right here in my house. In fact, there is a meeting tonight. Why don't you come?'

'Well, I don't know ...'

'I'm sure you will get much better results if you trust God rather than gypsy magic,' Catalina insisted. 'What can it hurt to try?'

Paulina pondered the suggestion, deciding finally to accept Catalina's invitation. That night, she came to the meeting and at the close of the service, asked the believers to pray for her and her surviving daughter. They did. For the next several weeks, Paulina Centeno attended every service in the Leons' living room. She brought her daughter along with her, as well. Soon, her husband began to accompany Paulina to church. Eventually, the entire Centeno family trusted Christ and were baptized. Their youngest daughter did not die. She did not even suffer an illness. The spell had been broken, just as Catalina Leon predicted.

Unfortunately, Catalina's career as an evangelist was nearing an untimely end. She began to feel unwell. Some mornings she was too tired to get out of bed. Her abdomen became distended as though she were pregnant, an impossibility since Catalina was long past child-bearing age. The family became alarmed and consulted doctors, who thought the problem was caused by a hernia. They wanted to operate immediately. The family consented, and Catalina underwent surgery.

After the operation, the doctors admitted to the Leons that they had misdiagnosed Catalina's illness. She was not suffering from a hernia, but rather a tumour in the uterus. 'We removed the malignancy,' the surgeon explained, 'and hopefully the cancer will not spread to other internal organs. But the prognosis is not good. The tumour weighed nine pounds.'

The surgery failed to cure Catalina. For a year she struggled with the cancer, living as a semi-invalid. When the family felt they could not give her adequate care at home she was hospitalized. Her condition continued to deteriorate. Convinced that death was imminent, Catalina asked to be taken home from the hospital. The family hesitated, still clinging to the hope that she might recover. Catalina had no such illusions, however. 'Don't worry about me dying,' she told Julia and Isabel during a visit to the hospital. 'After all, I don't have any good reason to go on living. You two are grown and married and have families of your own. You don't need me any more. This just means I will get to heaven ahead of the rest of you.'

She was adamant in her desire to die in her own bed. 'A hospital is no place to die,' she insisted. 'How can I commend my soul to God in this place?' She got her wish.

Cirilo Lopez came to see the Leons the day they brought Catalina home from the hospital. He said, 'Last night the Lord told me in a dream that you were passing through hard times. I was worried about you. You are like my family, my own children. I hope I can be of some help.' For next few weeks Cirilo came every day to read favourite texts of Scripture to Catalina and pray for her. He also administered medical treatments, drawing out the fluid that collected in her abdominal cavity with a large syringe. The simple operation helped to ease the intense pain Catalina was suffering.

One evening at church, Paulina Centeno took Julia aside. 'You had better prepare yourself,' she said. 'I don't think your mother will be here much longer. Last night in a dream, I saw a ladder descend from heaven to your house. Catalina climbed it and disappeared into the sky.'

The following afternoon, Julia went to awaken her mother from a nap. She had difficulty arousing Catalina and became alarmed that her mother had slipped into a coma. When Señora Leon finally awoke, she chided Julia for disturbing her. 'Why don't you leave me alone?' she pleaded gently. 'It is lovely to die. Like a deep dream that one cannot remember. Please just let me sleep.'

Catalina drifted off into unconsciousness once again, a peaceful expression radiating from her face. Later in the evening she sighed softly and drew her last breath. While Julia and Isabel wept at their mother's bedside, Catalina climbed the ladder that Paulina Centeno had seen in her dream.

* * *

By rights, Julia should have had time to mourn her mother's death before facing another crisis. But life deals tragedies at its own caprice. One month after Catalina passed away, the Colques' son José became critically ill. The sickness was sudden and unexpected. The little boy was near his second birthday and had always been a healthy child. If he had shown signs of an undernourished baby – listlessness, poor muscle coordination, inability to gain weight – then his parents might have foreseen a serious illness. But their plump and active toddler suffered no infirmity whatsoever until the fever struck.

Julia did what her mother had taught her to do to bring down José's temperature. She pumped the little one full of herbal teas and bathed him twice a day in cool water. But the home remedies did not help. Julia watched helplessly as the fever tormented her son. When he broke out in an angry rash, she decided to consult a doctor. 'This child is very sick,' he told Julia, his voice grave. 'You must keep him away from other children. This illness is contagious. It is called "scarlatina".'

The doctor said that José's condition was quite serious but there was hope of saving him. He advised Julia to discontinue the cold baths and prescribed medicine. But it proved too little, too late. Once again, dreams warned Julia of impending events. This time the visions were her own. One night, she dreamed that she sat with José in a brightly lit room. The little boy was crying and nothing Julia could do would comfort him. Julia's mother Catalina entered and said, 'Give José to me, I will put him to sleep.' Julia placed José in Catalina's arms. Her mother carried the little boy to a lovely white crib in the corner of the room and laid him in it. José's crying stopped. Julia immediately awoke.

In another dream, Julia was carrying José through the streets of a bright city. The pavement shone like polished crystal. The sky glowed golden, though no sun moved across it. As she neared a corner, her mother met her. 'Give me José,' she said. 'I want to carry him for a while.' Julia handed her son over to Catalina, who turned and disappeared around the corner. Immediately, Julia awoke. She lay gazing into the dark, trying not think about what the dreams portended.

The following day, José died.

The believers came to console Julia for the death of her little son. 'You must not take this too hard,' they encouraged her, 'José is with his grandmother now. Remember that he was always her favourite. She loved him so much that she took him to be with her.'

Julia felt in her heart that this was so. Nevertheless, the grief was unbearable. In the space of six weeks, she had lost her mother and her first-born child. The house where she had grown up, where she had known so much security and joy, which had until now been filled with familiar family sounds, was quiet, empty and alien. The Highway Service sent Florencio to work on a project far from town. Six days of the week he had to live in a camp with his workmates. Julia had no one with whom to share her grief. She slipped into deep depression, afraid to be alone. She especially dreaded the nights in her bedroom. Her mother had occupied the same room before Julia was married and now her memory filled the chamber. José's clothing filled the bureau, so that every time Julia opened a drawer she relived the loss of her baby.

For a year, Julia was under the spell of unrelenting grief. She was by nature a shy person and withdrew further and further into herself. She lost her appetite, becoming thin and frail. She performed household chores with little of her characteristic energy. Julia would later recall few incidents from that dark time. But she did remember the day when her father Calixto was talking to her, looked her straight in the eye and said, 'Julia, let the dead be dead. We can't bring them back.'

At that moment, Julia felt herself awakening as from a dream. The familiar surroundings of her home came sharply into focus. The world took on shape and colour once more. Julia could see something that she had completely lost sight of: the future. Soon after that, she gave birth to her second son, Jonás. When Jonás was nearly two, their third boy, Abel, was born. Two years later, the Colques had their fourth child, also a boy. With Javier, the family was complete. Even had she been so inclined, Julia had no more time to grieve.

* * *

As their family expanded, Florencio and Julia faced a familiar problem: money. Like most young families, they did not have enough of it. Theirs was a simple lifestyle. The house they lived in had no indoor plumbing. Except for a two-burner gas stove, they owned no domestic appliances. They did not have a car. Their only recreation was the church work. Whenever they travelled, it was to a *junta*. The only time they ate in restaurants was on such trips. Otherwise, every *peso* of income went to feed and clothe their family.

The Colques coveted only one material possession. They dreamed of having a home of their own. Living with Julia's family had posed no problem for them as newlyweds, but now that their family numbered five, they needed more space. If they were to buy a house, they were going to have to pay cash for it. A family in the Colques' circumstances could never hope to secure a mortgage. Paying cash meant saving money. A lot of money. Much more money than they could ever hope to save from Florencio's modest salary as road builder.

Although Florencio had worked nearly ten years at the job, he had not advanced very far up the salary scale. This was not due to sloth or incompetence. In fact, his superiors considered him one of their most valuable employees. Florencio simply failed to do the one thing that guaranteed a promotion. He did not bribe the boss.

'The other men arrive late for work, or don't even show up some days, but they get away with it,' he explained to his wife. 'They just bring the foreman a gift of cigarettes or whisky and he excuses them. Then, when it comes time for the boss to recommend someone for a promotion, whoever gives him the largest "tip" gets the job. But I can't, in good conscience, do those things. It's wrong, it's dishonest.'

Julia understood the ethical dilemma Florencio faced. She also knew that the National Highway Service was not the only public enterprise with built-in corruption. Policemen bought their way up the ranks, as did most civil servants. Jobs from customs official to toll booth operator often went to the highest bidder. That was because these positions offered an opportunity to earn a substantial under-the-table income. School teachers could not afford to bribe administrators to give them jobs, thanks to the dismal pay scale for educators. However, students routinely bribed teachers to give them good marks. They did this either because they failed to perform academically or because the instructor refused them the grade they deserved unless he were properly compensated.

The Colques had learned that Jesus expected his followers to be honest. That was why Florencio refused to bribe his superiors to promote him. Nor did Julia press her husband to do so in order to gain a promotion that would earn him more money. Instead, the couple opted for another strategy to reach their goal of a new house. Julia went into business for herself. Her mother had taught her how to sew and Julia thought she could make some money sewing *polleras*, the billowy skirts fashionable among Andean women. She started sewing *polleras* six hours a day. On Oruro's two weekly market days, Julia packed up her stock of skirts and headed towards the town centre with her three young sons in tow. There she staked out a small patch of pavement among the other street vendors and sold her *polleras*.

Julia did well enough with *pollera* sales to enable her to rent a stall in the central market and install her sewing machine there. On days when business was slow, she used the spare time to add to her stock. Julia was eventually selling enough *polleras* to support the family with her income. The couple put Florencio's earnings in the bank. By the time Jonás started school, they had saved enough money to buy a plot of land on Cañada Strongest Street, just a few doors up from Calixto Leon. Now they started saving money for adobe bricks, cement and timber to build a house.

Julia embarked on a second business career. A young couple in La Paz was getting married and named the Colques godparents of the wedding cake. It fell to Julia to negotiate the contract with a local cake maker, ordering the right size, style and flavour of cake. What she learned from the deal interested her, especially when she calculated how much the cake maker earned in wages and commission. Julia decided she would learn to make wedding cakes. She enrolled in night school and, for three years, studied cake making. She demonstrated enthusiasm and skill and graduated at the top of her class. She found that clients were plentiful, especially for an evangelical cake maker. The many believers whom Cirilo Lopez joined in wedlock at the Oruro church or in rural *juntas* supplied Julia with so much business that she found herself with little time ftor sewing. She closed her stall in the central market. From then on, she sewed only custom *polleras* for select clients.

Eventually, Julia was earning enough money from baking and sewing that the couple found they could save a portion of her income along with Florencio's. Theis meant the day when they could move into their own home would come even sooner. Florencio and Julia bolstered their household income with yet a third enterprise, farming. Julia's family owned a plot of land in Tolapalca, the Leon's ancestral home. It was ideal for producing carrots and onions. The couple grew potatoes on Florencio's farm in Lequepalca. They consumed a portion of the produce themselves, sold the surplus and spent the extra cash on the construction material for their new home.

Florencio and Julia Colque contradicted the mistaken notion that Latin Americans are lazy. With jobs, family and the Lord's work, their lives were a flurry of activity. Julia was in charge of running the household, of course, while Florencio was away on weekdays building highways. Normally, Julia devoted Mondays and Tuesdays to seamstress work and devoted the rest of the week to her wedding cake business. At weekends she helped her husband in church activities. Usually Florencio arrived home from the road camp late on Friday evenings. Often he found a group of believers, eager to discuss personal problems or church business, awaiting him in their inner courtyard patio. On Saturday mornings he travelled to a *junta*. There he spent the afternoon and evening preaching, counselling and praying for the sick. On Sundays he returned to Oruro in time for evening worship. At 6 a.m. on Mondays, he left by bus or train for the road camp, napping on the way to catch up on lost sleep. Vacations, of course, were different. Then, Florencio was off work for a month and, between weekend *juntas*, the family spent time in Tolapalca or Lequepalca working their fields of carrots, onions and potatoes.

In time, the Colques managed to build a two-storey house on the plot of land in Cañada Strongest Street. The five of them moved into the upper floor and lived in four rooms and a kitchen. The downstairs featured a storage room and a large hall. The hall was kept empty, except at weekends. Then believers from the *campo* came to town and the Colques' hall converted into one of the largest guest rooms in Oruro.

* * *

Francisca Lopez did not share her husband's zeal for religion. She accompanied Cirilo to church gatherings because she found it good business. Francisca ran a small grocery in Oruro and believers from the *campo* were her principal suppliers of potatoes, mutton and woollens. She also took merchandise with her to the *juntas* and sold to those in attendance. Señora Lopez believed that Christianity had its advantages. But those who knew her would not have described Francisca as on fire for God.

Francisca and Cirilo had other differences and sometimes fought over them. Following one particularly nasty argument, Francisca announced that she was going to Cochabamba. She would be visiting their son who lived there and did not know when, or if, she would return. Cirilo was not alarmed. His wife had threatened to leave him before. But when two weeks passed with no word from her, Cirilo began to feel uneasy. He contacted his son, who was surprised to learn his mother was not in Oruro. 'She left here five days ago,' he told his father. 'She mentioned something about going to Argentina, but I assumed she would stop at home on her way.'

Cirilo went at once to see Florencio and Julia Colque.

'I must tell you what has happened,' he told them anxiously. 'Francisca has gone to Argentina.'

'What for?' Florencio asked.

'I don't know,' Cirilo answered. 'I suppose she has her reasons, but she didn't tell me what they were.'

'You mean to say that she left without telling you?' Julia asked.

'Yes.'

Florencio and Julia exchanged worried glances. This was a serious problem.

'You must not tell anyone at the church about her disappearance,' Cirilo urged them. 'If the believers ask, tell them that she is visiting relatives, that she may be gone for some time. But we can't tell them the truth. It would ruin my ministry.'

The three friends were silent for some minutes. Cirilo was deep in thought. Finally he spoke, measuring each word carefully as a man does when revealing a secret.

'Francisca and I were foolish to marry,' he began. 'We didn't even know one anther. I was young, living far from home, lonely and homesick. I just grabbed the first girl that came along and said "Look, do you want to get married?" Neither of us were believers at the time. Still, it was a stupid thing to do.'

He looked at the young couple intently. 'Now you know why I counselled you to pray and fast those three months before you married. I did not want you to make the same mistake as I did. That is why I ask all the young people in the church to wait three months, six months, as long as it takes for them to be really sure before they marry. I could not bear for them to be as unhappy as Francisca and I have been.'

'Do you want to know something else?' Cirilo asked, and as he did so he lowered his voice. 'Our marital problems were not serious until I began preaching the gospel in earnest. I'm convinced that this is the work of the devil. It is his way of avenging himself against me for the work I am doing for God.'

Florencio and Julia were silent for some moments. When they spoke again, it was to agree not to reveal the circumstances of Francisca's sudden disappearance to anyone in the church. Cirilo said that, once her anger cooled, he expected his wife to come home. She would not be gone long, he hoped. Julia served him a hot supper and Cirilo returned home, relieved to have shared his burden. Cirilo waited for several days for Francisca to return. Days stretched into weeks and weeks into months. The vigil began to take its toll on the evangelist. His patience wore thin when he was called upon to manage crises in the church. He did less praying for healing than usual. Julia noticed that he no longer received messages from God through dreams. Worst of all, the believers were beginning to distrust Cirilo. They suspected that he was not telling the whole story about Francisca's disappearance. Finally, the Colques called the pastor to their home.

'You are going to have to do something, Brother Cirilo,' they urged him. 'It has been months since Francisca left and we can't cover it up any longer.'

'What can I do?' Cirilo wondered. 'I don't know where she is.'

'You can go to look for her,' they responded. 'Your vacation is coming up soon, isn't it? You must go to Argentina and find Francisca. The Lord will help you.'

Cirilo was sceptical but the Colques insisted. After much discussion, he agreed to their plan. Personally he believed the chances were nil of finding Francisca in a foreign country. On the other hand, it would give him something better to do than hang around an empty house. Florencio and Julia accompanied Cirilo to the station and saw that he got on the proper train. Cirilo left in melancholy mood. Like the prophet Hosea, he was going off to search for a truant wife who, even if found, might very well refuse to come home.

At Villazón on the Argentine border, Cirilo disembarked and began his search. He described Francisca to the ticket clerks and asked if they had remembered seeing her. Yes, they said, such a woman had been through there some time before. She had stayed a few weeks in the station selling *empanadas* (savoury pastries) to earn her passage into the interior of Argentina. When a group of migrant farm workers came through on their way to work on plantations there, she went with them. Cirilo was relieved to find that Francisca was travelling in a large company of Bolivians. It would be easier to trace a whole group of foreigners through Argentina than a single woman. He was unable to cross the border that day, so he decided to seek out an evangelical church and perhaps to find lodging for the night.

The church he found was holding a prayer service that evening. Cirilo described his quest to the small assembly and asked them to pray that he would find Francisca. After the service, some women came up to him with interesting news. They knew his wife, they said. She had attended services at the same church while she stayed in Villazón. Before she left with the migrant workers, she had told them she was bound for Orán. Encouraged by this information, Cirilo bought a ticket the next day for Orán. When he arrived in the town, he asked the railway workers if they had seen some farm labourers travelling with a middle-aged woman. Yes, one of the clerks remembered the group. No, he did not know where they had gone, but he guessed it would have been one of the plantations in the Chaco. For some days, Cirilo made his way from one plantation to the next, asking for information about his wife. Finally, he encountered the Bolivian migrant workers who had been travelling with Francisca. She had left the plantation, they said. She could not stand the heat. Orán enjoyed a cooler climate, due to its higher elevation, so she had returned there to find employment.

When Cirilo returned to Orán, the trail suddenly went cold. No one in the train station could give him any information about Francisca. He searched for her in all the central stores, but none of the employees knew her. Did he have a picture? Maybe the police could help him. No, thank you, Cirilo replied. It was not necessary to trouble the police in this case. He spent nearly a week canvassing the town. Finally, weary and discouraged, he concluded that his search was futile. He had been a fool to attempt it in the first place, he thought. Argentina was a huge country. Compared to Oruro, Orán was an immense city. What had made him think he could find

Francisca in this place? He decided he might as well return home, so he wandered back to the train station to buy his passage.

After purchasing his ticket, he sat down on a bench to rest. He watched a well-dressed young woman cross the platform, followed by her maid carrying the day's groceries home from the market. Cirilo glanced at the servant woman. She was middle-aged, stout and wore her grey-black hair in long braids. Cirilo looked more closely. Could it be? He hardly dared believe so, but there was no mistake. The maid was Francisca.

Cirilo ran up to his wife, calling her name excitedly. She stopped and looked around to see who it was. Her jaw dropped and she stood staring at her husband. The well-dressed young woman also stopped to see who was delaying her maid. Cirilo and Francisca began talking rapidly in Quechua. Her puzzled employer interrupted them and demanded to know what was going on.

'Pardon me, Señora,' Cirilo said apologetically. 'This is my wife.'

Now the well-dressed young woman stood, gaping, while Cirilo explained to her the circumstances of his search for Francisca. He finished by saying that he wanted to take his wife back to Oruro with him, if it was all right with her employer. The young woman answered that it was okay with her if Francisca herself wanted to go. Cirilo drew his wife aside to talk privately. Cirilo spoke to her in low whispers, in Quechua. He had to stop at intervals because of his weeping. Francisca answered his questions, also in Quechua, also weeping. At the end of the conversation, Cirilo accompanied Francisca and her employer to the young woman's house, carrying the groceries for them. Later, he returned to the train station and bought another ticket for Bolivia. Francisca was coming home.

* * *

The church that Cirilo Lopez presided over in Oruro was now quite large. So large, in fact, that no private living room nor rented storefront would accommodate the crowds that assembled for weekly meetings. All the members agreed that they needed to buy property of their own.

As they discussed the question among themselves, Cirilo insisted on two points. First, he urged the believers to buy a place on Cañada Strongest Street. 'This is where our work began and where it has thrived,' he said. 'People expect us to be here.' Second, he advised them to register the property titles in his name. 'Evangelical churches have few legal rights. The government could, at any moment, expropriate our real estate and we would have no recourse. If I am registered as the sole owner, they will not pay any attention to us.' As with all decisions in the church, Cirilo's instructions were carefully obeyed.

Instead of an empty lot, the believers opted to buy a large house. With extensive remodelling, it served three purposes: a meeting hall for the church, living quarters for the Lopez family and a grocery shop for Francisca. The Oruro church could never have acquired the prime piece of real estate with the local congregation's resources alone. To finance the venture, Cirilo levied a quota on every family in the national church. *Campesinos* were expected to donate a lamb. Urban households could give the equivalent value in cash. People were eager to help because, as Cirilo reminded them, they were giving to God, not man. Cirilo himself contributed substantially to the project. The largest, single donation came from Homer and Elvira Firestone.

By the time the church had moved into its spacious new building, they had registered incorporation papers with the Department of Culture in La Paz. The network of rural and urban churches that Cirilo Lopez and Homer Firestone had built was now a legally recognized religious body known as the 'Association of Evangelical Congregations'. Legal incorporation meant that the Bolivian government guaranteed Association members the right to freely practise their faith without restriction. Incorporation also meant the national church could engage in business transactions, such as the purchase and sale of real estate held in the name of the Association.

Scores of local churches had been established and the momentum of growth continued. The two Firestone children, now married with families of their own, had returned to Bolivia. Both Ron Firestone and his sister, LeTaye, were licensed chiropractors. The young couples were expanding the work of *Clínica El Libertador* and planned to carry on the work of Homer and Elvira when the elder Firestones should retire.

When it came to the question of who would succeed Cirilo Lopez, however, the answer was not so simple. His own sons might have been candidates. In good Latin American tradition, the mantel of leadership naturally passed from father to son. But a fundamental flaw disqualified the younger Lopezes from following in Cirilo's footsteps. They were not believing Christians. This fact was a source of embarrassment for Cirilo. Once, when he was visiting the church in La Paz, Pastor Mario Quispe publicly criticized Cirilo for his failure to bring his family into the faith. 'How can you care for the church of God if your own children do not even believe?' Mario asked him from the pulpit. Cirilo could give no answer. He was familiar with the text from 1 Timothy upon which Mario Quispe based his admonition. Cirilo could not argue with Scripture.

Florencio and Julia often heard him speak of his children's unbelief and weep. 'The greatest sadness of my life,' he said, 'is that I have not been able to serve the Lord in my house. Thousands of people have been converted in this work and for that I am grateful. But I still can't understand why God has not seen fit to save my family as well.' Cirilo had read in the Old Testament the story of Eli and empathized with the old priest's agony over his apostate sons.

Few persons, least of all Cirilo, were worrying over the problem of succession just yet. He was still in his prime and could anticipate many more years of useful life. But one day, Cirilo was having his hair cut and the barber scratched a mole on his temple. The wound bled profusely. The odd injury concerned Cirilo and he consulted a doctor for treatment. The doctor removed the mole but failed to do a biopsy on the tissue. Had he done so, he would have discovered that this was no ordinary blemish. It was a melanoma tumour. Melanoma is one of the fastest spreading cancers known to medical science. It wasted no time on Cirilo. Within a few weeks after the fateful haircut, his health had begun to deteriorate. Cirilo lost weight and suffered painful headaches. His robust energy diminished. Although he said nothing to anyone, the evangelist suspected he was dying. Accordingly, he took measures to prepare the church for his departure.

As was their custom, on the first Sunday of the quarter, the Oruro believers ascended a deserted peak outside the city to fast and pray. Their pastor led them up the mountain with a weary step. Still the congregation did not perceive that this would be the last such procession Cirilo would lead. At the close of the prayer vigil, the group gathered together to sing hymns and hear Cirilo preach. Cirilo told the assembly that he had an important announcement to make.

'You all know that God has raised up this church,' he said. 'It is not the work of men, nor of any one man. Nevertheless, God saw fit to give me a special responsibility in this work. Lately, I have been giving some thought as to who should take my place when I have gone on.'

'Since my sons are unbelievers, they cannot, of course, continue my work. I had thought one of my godchildren might follow in my footsteps. But it seems they have all gone after the world. That leaves one other. One who has been with us from the beginning, who has been faithful in his duties and who has the qualifications, according to 1 Timothy 3, to care for the church of God. That one is Florencio Colque.'

As Cirilo said this, he looked about the crowd for signs that the people were in agreement with his decision. Some were nodding their heads, others registered their assent with earnest 'Amens'. Cirilo was satisfied that the congregation confirmed his choice.

'Florencio, come here,' he said.

Florencio stepped up to Cirilo, who told him to kneel. Cirilo placed his Bible on the young man's head and started to pray. He asked God to anoint Florencio with his Spirit and to empower him to do great works. He prayed that men would always esteem Florencio for his faithfulness to Jesus Christ. Cirilo finished, Florencio stood up and the two men embraced.

Cirilo left the mountain that day with a sense of relief. He felt that a great weight had lifted from his shoulders. Whatever the future held for him personally, he was now prepared to face it. Paul's words in his second letter to Timothy expressed Cirilo's feelings. 'I have fought the good fight, I have finished the race, I have kept the faith. Henceforth there is laid up for me the crown of righteousness, which the Lord, the righteous judge, will award to me on that Day (2 Timothy 4.7–8).'

Florencio left the hill with a different feeling, a serious, solemn feeling. The great weight that was lifted from Cirilo's shoulders had passed directly onto his.

8

Pastor and Peacemaker

Homer Firestone had contemplated what would happen to the Association of Evangelical Congregations after Cirilo Lopez was gone. He recognized that Cirilo, a strong, somewhat autocratic leader, had been just the man to nurture the movement through its infancy. Until now, the Association of Evangelical Congregations had resisted the tendency to fragment because of its firm loyalty to Cirilo. But when he was no longer in charge, the church could splinter into petty factions. Dr Firestone also foresaw the potential problem of proselytism. Cirilo protected the flock from 'sheep stealers' – unscrupulous pastors and evangelists of other churches who sought to lure the believers into their own denominations. Such tactics, apart from being unethical, sowed discouragement in local congregations. Christians sometimes became so confused by the pestering that they abandoned the evangelical faith altogether. Homer Firestone knew that if the national movement were to survive intact, the focus of its allegiance would have to shift.

During the time Homer was pondering this dilemma, he and Elvira received visitors from North America. The Missionary Board of the Church of God was interested in beginning mission work in Bolivia and heard of *Clínica El Libertador*. Mission executives thought the property might serve as a base for their projected outreach, so they travelled from Anderson, Indiana, to Cochabamba and talked with the Firestones about purchasing *Clínica El Libertador*. During the course of the conversation, Homer and Elvira happened to mention their involvement with

Cirilo Lopez and the indigenous church. Their description of the Bolivian church's beliefs and practices intrigued the Church of God representatives. By the end of their talks with Homer and Elvira, they had changed their minds about buying *Clínica El Libertador*. Instead, they proposed an affiliation between the Association of Evangelical Congregations and the Church of God.

The Firestones responded to the overture with caution. They promised to speak to Cirilo and other leaders about the merger proposal, but could not guarantee a positive response. They pointed out that Cirilo had long been wary of ties to foreigners and would not easily be persuaded to surrender the church's autonomy.

Meanwhile, the Firestones availed themselves of opportunities to become better acquainted with the Church of God. Elvira's brother, Vernon Englund, pastored a Church of God congregation in California and their son, Ron, had attended the Glendale Church of God while serving on the faculty of the Los Angeles College of Chiropractic. Homer and Elvira soon discovered that this North American church had much in common with the Association of Evangelical Congregations in Bolivia. Both, for example, held strong convictions regarding personal holiness and the Spirit-filled life. Both organizations adhered to congregational church government. The Firestones discovered that the Church of God even practised foot-washing, considering it an ordinance on a par with baptism and communion. The churches in Bolivia held foot-washing services monthly.

Despite the close compatibility of the two church bodies, however, Elvira harboured reservations about the merger. She sought a clear word from the Lord on the issue. That word came one day as she was reading Acts 10, the account of Peter's visit to the Roman centurion, Cornelius. Reluctant to associate with Gentiles, the apostle would have refused to go with the messengers that Cornelius sent to fetch him. But a dramatic message from God overcame his reservations. 'Rise and go down, and accompany them without hesitation; for I have sent them.' When she read those words, Elvira knew immediately that this message was for her. She told Homer that God had ordained the merger plan and would see it succeed.

The Firestones began to take steps to bring together the Church of God and the Association of Evangelical Congregations. They arranged for Cirilo Lopez and other leaders in Oruro to meet with executives of the Church of God Missionary Board to discuss affiliation. Cirilo expressed interest in the plan but did not commit himself to the merger. Not long after that meeting, he took to his bed. The moment was fast approaching when the Bolivian church would find itself bereft of Cirilo's leadership.

The Firestones decided to contract a mission plane to carry Cirilo to Sucre for consultation with a specialist. The couple sat together in the doctor's waiting room when the physician announced his diagnosis. 'Our tests indicate that Señor Lopez has malignant melanoma cancer,' he told them. 'The initial tumour has metastasized to the brain, making further treatment impossible.'

'No, Doctor, you can't be serious!' Elvira blurted out, trembling. 'Not that!' Because of her years of experience as a nurse, she understood too well the implications of the diagnosis.

'We have checked and re-checked all the data,' the doctor answered. 'There is no mistake.' He paused. 'I can't see that it would do any good for us to inform Señor Lopez of the results. I'm afraid the only thing you can do for him now is to take him back home to die.'

Elvira wept. She understood what an agonizing death Cirilo faced.

Back in Oruro, the believers rallied to support their leader in his struggle against the cancer. Money poured in from La Paz, Kami, Lequepalca and many other towns to help defray medical costs. But in spite of the believers' efforts on his behalf, Cirilo's condition continued to deteriorate. The church braced itself for the end.

* * *

One man who was especially active during the final days of Cirilo's life was Valerio Montalvo. Valerio's aggressive personality and talent for preaching had made him a reputation. The believers recognized him as a capable leader. All this was fine enough, except that Valerio wanted to be *the* leader. That Cirilo had publicly designated Florencio Colque for that role galled Valerio. He decided to challenge Florencio for the office of heir apparent. Valerio found an ally in Ramón Titicala. The two of them plotted an ingenious *coup* against an unsuspecting Florencio.

Their plan began with daily visits to Cirilo Lopez's bedside. 'I can't understand why you anointed Florencio to take over the work,' Valerio told the dying man. 'The people certainly do not want him.' At first, Cirilo paid little attention to Valerio. He was confident he had made the right choice. Nevertheless, Valerio's repeated allusions to widespread discontent with Florencio eventually awakened a doubt in Cirilo's mind. To this piece of misinformation, Valerio added another. 'Beware of Florencio,' he repeatedly warned Cirilo. 'After you are gone, he is planning to take this church away from you and give it to the *gringos*.'

Had Cirilo been in possession of his full mental faculties at that point, he might have detected Valerio's cunning. But the cancer had severely reduced his capacity to make rational judgements. Insecurities began to haunt the dying man. Because Florencio was away at the road camp all week and continually preaching at *juntas* on weekends, he was unable to visit Cirilo himself. When he did finally appear at his mentor's bedside, he received a cool reception. Florencio was puzzled by this, but it did not distract him from the business he wanted to discuss with Cirilo.

'Brother Cirilo, you have given me a great responsibility,' he began, 'and I feel very much like a child. You must teach me, give me some of your wisdom. Otherwise, I will surely fail.'

'No, Florencio,' Cirilo responded, 'I cannot teach you what you need to know. I have no more strength for it. You will have to learn by yourself. The Lord will be your teacher.'

Cirilo's refusal unsettled Florencio. He was beginning to feel the heavy weight of leadership more each day and hoped Cirilo might give him a sympathetic hearing. 'Please do this much, at least,' Florencio urged. 'The brethren have elected me president of the board of directors. That makes me responsible for managing church properties. While there is still time, we must register the titles to this building in the name of the Association of Evangelical Congregations. May I have the documents now so that I can make the transfer?'

For a brief moment, Cirilo frowned. 'If I were you, son, I wouldn't worry about all that,' he answered. 'You don't need this house. You concentrate on spiritual matters and let the material things take care of themselves.'

Cirilo's evasive reply did not satisfy Florencio. The building in which the Lopez family lived and where the Oruro congregation worshipped had been purchased with church offerings, he reminded Cirilo. It was therefore only proper that the titles list the Association as the legitimate owner. Cirilo agreed that the national church was the legitimate owner. No one was disputing that, he said. But he insisted that the titles remain in his name for political reasons.

'As it stands, this chapel is classified as a public cooperative,' he told Florencio. 'Do you know why? I'll tell you why. Let's say a communist government were to take over Bolivia. The first thing they would do would be to close down all the churches and confiscate their buildings. We would lose everything. But, if we are recognized as a cooperative, they would not touch us. Communists are the world's greatest promoters of cooperatives.'

'In the meantime, Florencio, you must not worry about these things,' Cirilo continued. 'My wife Francisca and my sons will administer the material aspects of the church and you will be free to look after the spiritual needs.'

Florencio decided not to press the issue, afraid that the controversial topic might aggravate the dying man's suffering. He changed the subject. Later, however, as he was walking home from the interview, it occurred to Florencio that Cirilo's refusal to deliver the property titles might be due to mistrust. Perhaps Lopez suspected that Florencio, once he got his hands on the titles, would try to expropriate the building by registering the titles in his own name. The young man had no such intention, of course. To prove it, he decided to visit Cirilo the following day and insist that Cirilo himself handle all the details of the transfer.

Cirilo was unhappy to see Florencio the next afternoon. When Florencio brought up the question of the property titles a second time, Cirilo did not hide his displeasure.

'Why do you want those titles?' he snapped. 'Don't you trust me? I have built this work from the ground up, no one has a right to question my integrity.' Half rising from his bed he pointed at the door. 'If you have no more confidence in me than that, Florencio Colque, there's the door!'

Stunned, Florencio rose to leave. He had never expected this kind of reaction from Cirilo. Before he could reach the exit, the sick man added a second jolt.

'I have made a mistake,' Cirilo said to Florencio. 'I never should have appointed you as my successor. You are not the man to take over my work.'

To Florencio, these words were like a hard blow to the stomach. Later that day, Cirilo did something that would cause Florencio more hurt. When Valerio Montalvo arrived for his daily visit, he was ushered into Cirilo's room and commanded to kneel by his bedside. Laying his hands on Valerio's head, the dying man consecrated him as the one to carry on in his footsteps.

* * *

Like Florencio, Homer Firestone had difficulty finding time for a visit to Cirilo's bedside. But knowing that little time remained for his friend, Dr Firestone took a day from his busy schedule to travel to Oruro. Cirilo greeted him warmly and invited him to drink a cup of tea. The two men reminisced about times past, such as the month Cirilo spent in Cochabamba, helping Homer build the *Clínica El Libertador* by day and studying the Bible with him each night. The two also recalled the many trips they had made together to distant *juntas*, the bone-jarring travel, the occasional dangers, the practical jokes. Dr Firestone mentioned the pending merger with the Church of God in North America and asked Cirilo his opinion of the arrangement. 'Of course I am in favour of this merger,' Cirilo assured Homer. 'You are right when you say that this will save our work from division and proselytism. You can count on my unconditional support.'

Homer touched on another important issue. 'Cirilo, it's time to do something about the titles to this building,' he said, gently. 'You know that if you should die with the property still registered in your name, it would pass directly to your children. The church has no legal document proving that it is the rightful owner. Now, let's say your sons decide that they don't want the church using the chapel any more. They could evict us and we would have no recourse. Brother Cirilo, you don't want that to happen, do you?'

'Of course not!' Cirilo declared. 'Brother Homer, I appreciate your concern for this piece of land,' he added earnestly. 'You are right to insist that we register the property in the name of the church. Even though I do not think my sons would ever abuse the believers, I will set things right so that there will be no problem. You have my word on it.'

Homer had never had any reason to distrust Cirilo. His solemn promise allayed Dr Firestone's worries that the church property would pass into the wrong hands. He left the dying man's room that day confident that Cirilo would transfer the titles to the Association before his death.

Two weeks later, the believers gathered in the chapel on Thursday night for their customary prayer meeting. The meeting proceeded in the usual manner. An hour of congregational singing was followed with a devotional reading from the Scriptures. Then came more congregational singing, a message, group prayer and spontaneous testimonies. But this particular Thursday night meeting ended like no other. Before the closing hymn, Valerio Montalvo and Ramón Titicala entered, carrying Cirilo Lopez on a litter. The two men also carried a letter they asked to read to the congregation. It was, in effect, an order to sever all ties between the church and Homer and Elvira Firestone, immediately and irrevocably. The letter also strictly forbade further contact with Mario Quispe, pastor of the church in La Paz. Cirilo Lopez's signature appeared at the bottom of the document. A hush fell over the congregation after the reading. Cirilo indicated that he wanted to address the believers. He was too weak to stand, nearly too weak to speak. Valerio held a microphone to his lips so that the crowd could hear.

'Brethren, you must not work with the North Americans any more,' Cirilo said, faintly. 'They are too powerful. Once I am gone, they will dominate the church and no one will be able to stop them. As for Mario Quispe, he has studied in a seminary and uses the title "pastor". You must never work with a pastor because, sooner or later, he will insist you pay him a salary. From now on, you must keep your distance from pastors and missionaries. Otherwise, you will fall back into the same errors that we came out of years ago.'

This was the man's last message to the congregation in Oruro. Before the believers gathered for their next Thursday night prayer meeting, Cirilo Lopez was dead.

* * *

Homer Firestone was working in his office in *Clínica El Libertador* when Cirilo's daughter, who lived in Cochabamba, rang the doorbell. 'Thank goodness you're still here!' she gasped, breathlessly. 'Everybody else is already gone.'

'Gone? Gone where?' Homer asked.

'To Oruro, of course,' the young woman replied. 'I've been running all over the city looking for someone to take me there. I thought surely I would miss the funeral. Can I go with you? You will take me with you, won't you?'

Homer realized what had happened. Without revealing to Cirilo's daughter that he did not know of her father's death, he assured her that she could accompany them to Oruro. He then informed his wife of the news and Elvira hurriedly made preparations for the journey. Ron Firestone and his wife, Violet, would join them. Once on the road, the Firestone family speculated as to why no one had informed them, either by phone or telegram, of Cirilo's death. Since the rest of the believers in Cochabamba had been notified, the Firestones suspected someone in Oruro meant to snub them. But why? They knew nothing of the events in Oruro prior to Cirilo's death, but sensed something was amiss. Fearing their late start might cause them to miss Cirilo's funeral, the family drove all night to arrive at the service on time.

Because embalming is not generally practised in Bolivia, the law requires that the deceased be buried within 24 hours of death. As a result, most funerals are poorly attended affairs. However, the news of Cirilo Lopez's death travelled quickly through the countryside. Believers arrived *en force* in Oruro the following day. Three thousand people gathered to mourn Cirilo's passing, making his was one of the largest funerals the city had ever seen.

The Firestones arrived in time for Homer to preach the memorial sermon. Afterward, he led the huge procession to the cemetery. When they arrived there, Valerio Montalvo insisted on delivering the graveside message, in Quechua, with no Spanish translation. The rest of the church leaders, embarrassed by this affront, thrust Valerio aside and invited Dr Firestone to deliver the final eulogy. The awkward scene confirmed the missionaries' suspicions that all was not well. Upon returning from the cemetery, Homer and Ron asked to meet with the deacons of the Oruro church. Uneasy tension pervaded the meeting during the first few minutes. The deacons told the Firestones about the letter that had been presented to the Oruro church the previous Thursday night and described its contents. They explained that, at Cirilo's request, they had each signed the document.

'But we only did it because we knew Cirilo was dying,' they contended. 'We didn't want to embarrass him in front of the congregation. The man was out of his head.' They assured the Firestones that none of them had any intention of obeying the letter and unanimously agreed the church would continue working with the Firestone family.

Homer thanked the deacons for their vote of confidence. 'Only one more thing disturbs me,' he said, 'the question of the transfer of the church property. Cirilo died leaving the titles in his name.

We must transfer ownership as soon as possible to protect the church's interests.'

The deacons responded that, in their opinion, this would not be a problem because the Lopez family was fully trustworthy. 'Nevertheless,' Dr. Firestone insisted, 'we must do things decently and in order. Are the titles in your possession?'

'No, they're not,' the deacons replied uneasily. 'But don't worry, we can get them from Cirilo's son, Antonio, any time we ask.'

'I suggest you get them as soon as possible,' Homer cautioned. The meeting adjourned.

Valerio Montalvo was not present that day to pledge his solidarity with the rest of the church leaders. He vowed to continue his campaign to wrest control of the Association of Evangelical Congregations from Florencio Colque, Homer Firestone or anyone else who threatened his position as the ordained heir to Cirilo Lopez. Valerio found more allies for the fight. Cirilo's brother, Alberto, suddenly appeared to lend support. Alberto Lopez pastored a church in the same denomination that Cirilo had abandoned 12 years earlier. He offered to help Valerio block the merger with the Church of God. 'It would be a crime for this work to be handed over to the *gringos*,' he asserted. 'This church belongs to *our* denomination. Cirilo was one of *us*.'

The annual general assembly of the Association was two months away. The three men knew this particular congress would be a crucial one. It would also provide them with the best opportunity to stage a *coup* against the Association leadership. They knew they must use to good advantage the time leading up to the congress. Valerio Montalvo and Ramón Titicala paid daily visits to families in the church. 'You must oppose this merger with the Church of God,' they urged the members. 'The missionaries are selling your souls to the *gringos*.' Despite fervid arguments, the two failed to convince many believers that affiliating themselves with an international movement was tantamount to selling their souls.

Alberto Lopez had slightly more success. 'The Church of God belongs to the World Council of Churches,' he confided ominously, and incorrectly, to anyone who would listen. Most believers had never heard of the Council, so Alberto described it to them. 'It's a Communist organization controlled by the Pope in Rome.'

Despite their failure to win widespread support among members of the Association, Valerio and his cohorts found strong allies who could eventually tip the balance of power in their favour. Francisca Lopez and her sons approved of Valerio's scheme to expel the Firestones. They also supported his bid to usurp Florencio Colque as Cirilo's successor. The Lopez sons had scarcely any contact with the church while their father lived. But now that Cirilo was gone, they felt an intense desire to see his final wishes obeyed. Valerio welcomed the Lopez family's assistance. They all agreed that their struggle would be difficult, perhaps unpleasant. However, they possessed two assets that gave them considerable leverage: legal title to the church building and the keys to the front door.

* * *

The General Assembly of the Association of Evangelical Congregations convened in Oruro in November 1974. Florencio Colque, President of the Board of Directors, presided. The delegates represented 70 local churches. Seated among the banks of merchants, truck drivers and *campesinos* were persons who, though not elected representatives, would have great impact on the Assembly's deliberations. Homer Firestone had never before attended the annual congress. His pledge to respect the right of Bolivian leaders to manage church affairs obliged him to decline the yearly invitation to the assembly. Ron Firestone, who accompanied his father to this congress, had never been present before, either. But the troubling events of the past weeks had persuaded the missionaries to break tradition and attend the congress. Also present for the first time that day were Cirilo Lopez's sons, Antonio and Elias. They had come to defend the church from foreigners, Communists and all other enemies of its rightful leader. The man who claimed that title, Valerio Montalvo, was conspicuously absent from the congress. He and Alberto Lopez were together in a downstairs room, awaiting the outcome of the proceedings.

The business meeting commenced with each local church submitting a progress report. The Board of Directors rendered accounts and the delegates discussed plans for the upcoming national *junta* at Lequepalca. Florencio Colque introduced Ron and Violet Firestone to the assembly, which unanimously approved the young couple to serve as missionaries to the Association alongside the senior Firestones.

The meeting was about to adjourn when a delegate asked in Quechua, 'Pardon my ignorance, but I heard something about a "letter of the deceased". They say that Brother Cirilo left instructions in this letter just before he died, but we in the *campo* can get no information about it. What is this all about?'

Elias Lopez was immediately on his feet. 'Yes!' he called out, 'what about that letter? According to that letter the church is supposed to separate itself from Pastor Mario Quispe as well as from all foreign missionaries!'

His outburst suddenly shattered the serene boredom of the business meeting. Elias launched into a bitter tirade. He blasted the church for disobeying his father's dying wish to expel the Firestones. He accused the Firestones of betraying the work his father had single-handedly built by turning it over to foreigners. Finally, he charged the Association of Evangelical Congregations with trying to steal the church property, 'from my family, who sacrificed so much to build it'.

Those who knew the Lopez family history could appreciate how preposterous were Elias's claims. Cirilo's youngest son had been something of a prodigal, leaving home to seek his fortune in Brazil. When word reached him that Cirilo had terminal cancer and wanted to see him, Elias opted to remain in Brazil. When he finally did return home, it was too late. Cirilo was already dead. But many of the delegates at the congress that day were unacquainted with Elias. His impassioned speech stirred them. Voices asked that the letter of the deceased be read publicly.

Froilan Colque rose to his feet and looked Elias Lopez directly in the eye. 'Young man, are you a believer?' he asked. The crowd hushed to hear Elias's response.

'No,' he said, barely audibly.

'Have you been baptized?' Froilan said.

Elias fidgeted. 'No.'

'If you are neither a believer nor baptized, then you are not a member of this Association. In fact, you have no right to be here in this congress.' Elias made no answer.

Froilan turned to the delegates. Speaking in Quechua, he recounted the story of his conversion to Christ. He described the sacrifices, hardships and dangers he had faced as a result of that decision. He also said that, if he had it all to do over again, he would change nothing. He was weeping as he told the story. 'I was saved, my life was changed, because of the gospel of Jesus Christ and because of this fellowship to which we belong. Homer Firestone is one of the founders. He is like a father to me. I will not turn my back on Brother Firestone now.'

Ramón Titicala saw that the tide of opinion was swinging to the opposition. He nudged Antonio Lopez, Elias's older brother. Antonio rose to his feet.

'But what about the letter of the deceased?' he cried. 'My father's letter was specific in its instructions. We are no longer to associate with missionaries or pastors.'

Mario Quispe's son, Victor, was losing his patience. He stood up and confronted Antonio. 'You are always talking about this letter,' he said, 'but none of us who are mentioned in the letter have seen it. Show us this letter, we want to see what it says.'

Antonio did not answer Victor, but sat down to confer with his associates. The delegates waited expectantly for Antonio to produce the letter. He did not. Instead, he lamely explained that the original, with Cirilo's signature, had been lost. The evasion convinced many of those present that either the letter did not exist, or Cirilo's signature on it had been forged.

Homer Firestone had said nothing during the entire meeting. At Florencio Colque's insistence, however, he now rose to address the delegates. The room fell silent as Homer talked about his long relationship with Cirilo and their work together to nurture the church from a handful of believers meeting in Alberto Conde's storefront to its present size and standing. He told about sacrifices many families had made to provide chapel buildings, including the one where they were meeting. He showed the delegates a receipt, signed by Cirilo, for a US$500 donation Homer and Elvira gave toward the purchase the property. Murmurs rippled through the assembly. The receipt indicated that the Firestones had invested more in the church property than anyone, including Cirilo's family.

Homer concluded his remarks. 'I have never shown this receipt before in public because I did not want to embarrass Cirilo. His friendship meant a great deal to me.' Homer's voice cracked. 'But if that friendship is to end in rejection and the church that we built together wishes me to leave, then I will leave.'

Unable to control his emotions any longer, Homer broke down and wept.

A moment of stunned silence followed. In all his memory, Ron Firestone had never witnessed his father crying. He realized the depth of Homer's feelings for the Bolivian believers. It was a scene the young man would never forget. For many of the delegates, the sight was unbearable. They were looking upon a good and godly man scorned. Homer Firestone's weeping shook them and they wept, as well.

Florencio Colque rose to his feet. He perceived that, except for a small minority, the delegates wanted to assure Dr Firestone and his family of their regard. 'Fellow believers,' Florencio said, 'you know that I was one of the first persons converted in this church. In the years that I have worked with Cirilo Lopez and Homer Firestone, I have learned an important lesson. True people of God exist in every country, they are of every race. We are rich for being part of that fellowship.' He paused. 'We cannot separate ourselves from Pastor Mario Quispe, nor from Dr Firestone. Our faith has no boundaries, our faith has no borders.'

Ramón Titicala, Antonio and Elias Lopez walked out of the congress. They realized their cause was lost. Nevertheless, the three hurled a parting challenge. 'All those who are true to Cirilo Lopez and what he stood for, follow us downstairs!' Few of the delegates responded to the appeal. Florencio adjourned the meeting. All items of business had been covered, all pending issues settled. Florencio's final word to the delegates was an invitation to attend Sunday worship at 10 a.m. the following morning.

As the delegates filed out of the building, they passed a room on the first floor where Valerio Montalvo, Ramón Titicala, Alberto Lopez and his nephews, Antonio and Elias, were meeting. Their deliberations lasted long into the night.

* * *

The next morning, believers from all over the city made their way to Cañada Strongest Street to attend worship. But that day no services were held at the chapel of the Association of Evangelical Congregations. The front door was locked.

The hour appointed for worship was long past when Antonio Lopez appeared at a second-storey window to address the crowd milling about in the street below. He told them that no one would be allowed to enter the building unless they pledged allegiance to the newly elected board of directors. The believers were surprised to hear that new officers had been elected and asked who they might be. Antonio ticked off the names: Valerio Montalvo, President; Maximo Huarachi, Vice-President; Ramón Titicala, Secretary; Antonio Lopez, Treasurer.

The believers in the street were appalled. They had not elected these men, they said, and would not accept them as leaders of the church. In that case, Antonio replied, they were no longer welcome on the premises. The believers protested, charging that no one had the right to shut them out of their own chapel. Antonio replied that he had every right to shut them out because he owned the building. He had the titles, legally registered in his name, to prove it. The believers fell silent. The chapel was no longer theirs? How could that be? Bewilderment gave way to anger as they realized that the man who was taking it from them had not invested one penny of his own money in the building. Some of the crowd gave vent to their rage, shouting threats at Antonio. One petite woman challenged him to settle accounts with his fists, if he were man enough.

Homer Firestone saw that the situation was becoming volatile. He suggested the believers move down the street and hold their Sunday service in the courtyard of Florencio and Julia Colque's home. The congregation sullenly complied. That afternoon, Homer, Ron and the Colques paid a visit to the Lopez family. The four tried to reason with Francisca and her sons. They reminded them that the funds to purchase the house and remodel the building had been given as offerings to the church. The property belonged to God, not man. If the Lopezes pressed their claim of ownership, they would be robbing not people, but God.

'All I know is that my father left us this property,' Elias Lopez shrugged. 'If my father wants to leave an inheritance to his children, who am I to question that?'

'But the property was in your father's name only for a legal safeguard,' Julia reminded him. 'He was going to register the house in the church's name before he died. He promised Dr Firestone he would.'

'That's not my problem,' Elias responded. 'You people should have taken care of this business while my father was still alive.' Cynically, he added, 'You will have to talk to my father about this. Why, he's in the cemetery right now. Go and complain to him there.'

The visitors realized the futility of continuing the interview, so they returned to the Colque home. There they huddled with the church elders and discussed their options for regaining their building. The majority wanted to take the case to court. They felt Dr Firestone's receipt for the US$500 would convince the judges that the Lopezes were not the rightful owners. Church leaders, angered by Valerio's duplicity, clamoured for justice. Homer and Ron listened quietly to the debate. When everyone had expressed their frustration, the missionaries asked to speak. They outlined the problems a legal battle would bring for the Association. They described the negative impact a bitter dispute would have on the believers and the damage it would cause to the church's public standing. They expressed their opinion that, even if the Association were to win in court, it would probably lose more than it stood to gain. They counselled the leaders to follow Jesus' advice and turn the other cheek.

'But what are we going to do for a church building?' the elders demanded. The Oruro congregation could not afford to purchase property on its own and, thanks to the current muddle, dare not ask believers in the *campo* for help. It would be years before the Oruro church could rebuild credibility with the *campesino* believers. Even more years would pass before they scraped enough money together to purchase property. The elders finished their litany of gloom. Homer spoke again, mentioning that he had foreseen the possibility of losing the Oruro property to the Lopez family. The Firestone family was prepared help the believers recover their losses, he said. He reached into his pocket, withdrew five US$100 bills and laid them on the table. 'This is my grain of sand,' he said.

Ron Firestone laid down US$500 beside his father's money. 'This is my offering for the new chapel,' he said. 'In addition, my family has decided to give US$1,000 from the income of *Clínica El Libertador*.' The Church of God in North America has offered US$500, as well. Brothers, do you think that with US$2,500, we can acquire a suitable plot of land on which to build our new chapel?'

For a moment, the elders were too astounded to reply. Of course this was enough to buy a new piece of land, they finally managed to say. Furthermore, they were sure that once the congregation learned of the Firestones' offering, the believers themselves would add substantially more to the fund. A ray of hope pierced the gloom hovering over the group. The elders could envision a new chapel, much larger than the one they had lost, filled to capacity with worshippers. After all, God had raised up this church. They could trust him to preserve it.

* * *

By forfeiting the Oruro chapel, the believers avoided a long legal battle that would have absorbed time and resources. That was good. They were going to need all the time and resources they could afford just to hold the church together. A month after the momentous meeting in Oruro, Homer and Elvira had to return to California to be with their daughter LeTaye, who was critically ill. They would be absent for nearly a year, leaving the work of *Clínica El Libertador* to Ron and Violet. Before he left, Homer asked his son to visit as many *juntas* as he could fit in between his six-days-a-week chiropractic schedule. 'Someone must continue the healing ministry now that Cirilo is gone,' Homer explained. 'You are the one to do that.'

'Your visits can also do a great deal to keep local churches from leaving the Association,' Homer told Ron. 'I doubt that we have heard the last of Valerio Montalvo and his group. Who knows what kind of tricks they will pull. You will have a lot of fires to put out.'

Homer said more than he knew. Valerio Montalvo was indeed setting fire to the churches. One incident involved the congregation in Sorocachi. The believers in the small Altiplano village were divided. Half wanted to follow Valerio and his band, but half opted to remain with the Association. The sticking point was their chapel. They could not decide to which group it should belong since both parties had an equal share in it. The debate between the rival groups became so rancorous that non-believers in the community gossiped about the rift, snickering about the meek evangelicals suddenly turned pugnacious. For his part, Valerio Montalvo decided on a simple solution to the Sorocachi problem. The chapel was causing the problem, therefore the chapel must go. One night, he arrived in the village with a quantity of dynamite and tossed the charge through the window of the empty church. A deafening roar and a cloud of smoke abruptly ended the argument over the chapel.

Florencio Colque's tactics were decidedly less incendiary than his rival's. Some weeks after the controversial 1974 congress, he visited the church in Yauricoya. Before they allowed him to preach, local elders took Florencio aside and inquired about his standing in the Association of Evangelical Congregations. They said that Valerio had come to Yauricoya and told them that he was the legitimate president now, that Florencio was an imposter. Florencio saw the *campesinos* were genuinely perplexed about whom to believe. He decided to force the issue.

'Despite Brother Valerio's claim, there has been no change in the Board of Directors,' he said. 'I am still the President and the Association still endorses the Firestone family as our missionaries. It is true that Valerio wants the church to recognize him as its leader. He says this was Cirilo Lopez's dying wish.'

Florencio paused. 'Brothers, you have a decision to make. Are you going to maintain your relationship with me, the other elected leaders of the Association and the Firestone family, or are you going to follow Valerio? It's up to you.'

The Yauricoya elders withdrew to discuss the question among themselves. Before Florencio left for Oruro that night, they informed him of their decision. 'For many years, since we first heard the gospel from you and Froilan, we have known you as men we can trust. We know Dr Firestone and his son, Ronaldo, are trustworthy men, too. As for Valerio Montalvo, we cannot be sure what kind of a president he will be. Therefore, we will maintain our relationship with you and the Firestones.'

For two years, leaders of the Association of Evangelical Congregations engaged in negotiations like this with churches throughout the *campo*. Ron Firestone would remember two critical factors that determined the success of the struggle to hold the organization together. First, was prayer, especially the prayers of Elvira and Violet Firestone. The two women made the preservation of the Association a central theme of their daily conversations with God. Second, was the *corps* of gifted Bolivian leaders that stepped in to share the leadership of the church. For all his genius, Cirilo Lopez had lacked the ability to delegate authority. Now that he was gone, a dozen decision-makers shared oversight of the movement Cirilo had initiated.

Mario Quispe and his son Victor, played a key role in guiding the church through the confusion following Cirilo's death. The Quispes worked to secure incorporation papers for the Association to replace the documents that Valerio Montalvo had confiscated. Because they lived near the capital, the Quispes were able to push the normally sluggish process through government bureaucracy in just two years. In 1976, the Bolivian Government ratified the new national organization, now known as the 'Association of the Church of God, Reformed'. The official act finalized the affiliation between the Bolivian church and the Church of God in North America.

By this time, the Association had nearly recovered from the division suffered two years earlier. The perpetrators of that division, however, did not fare so well. Following the controversial 1974 congress, Señora Francisca Lopez and her family prohibited worship services on their property in Cañada Strongest Street for six months. When the chapel finally reopened, few worshippers occupied the pews. Valerio Montalvo's appeal as a preacher had waned. His coalition had disintegrated, as well. Elias Lopez returned to Brazil. Alberto Lopez went back to his own church, having failed to 'restore' the 70 congregations of the Association to his denomination. Ramón Titicala lost interest in religion altogether.

Yet, at the Colque home several doors up the street, a large crowd continued to squeeze into the courtyard each week for Sunday worship. Each year during Holy Week, believers from churches all over the *campo* still gathered for the annual *junta* in Lequepalca. There, Florencio Colque, Homer and Ron Firestone, Mario and Victor Quispe and dozens of other evangelists still preached to several thousand believers on Easter weekends.

9

Neighbours

For five years, the believers in Oruro met for worship in private homes. Though they had raised enough money to purchase land for a new church building, they were undecided about what to do with the funds. The church had always met on Cañada Strongest Street and the members hoped to build a new chapel there, but all the property on that street already had owners. Some thought the church should move to the edge of the city where land was cheap and plentiful. Others said too many members would lose touch if the congregation left its familiar neighbourhood. Marcos Arze, who lived two doors down from Florencio and Julia Colque, provided the solution. He offered to divide in half the property he owned. Marcos would live on one side and sell the other portion to the church. The congregation bought the parcel of land. The Missionary Board of the Church of God raised US$5,000 for construction; the believers added an equal amount themselves. Work began on a two-storey building. When it was completed in 1979, it was the first chapel in Bolivia registered in the name of the Association of the Church of God, Reformed.

It was also the first chapel on Cañada Strongest Street since before Julia Colque was born. In the 1940s, Doña Consuelo installed her brothel on the street and the establishment had flourished. When Consuelo died, her maid took over the business. As often happens in commerce, the lucrative enterprise attracted competitors. Two more houses of prostitution opened for business on either side of the Colques' home. Cañada Strongest Street became the heart of Oruro's red-light district. Now, it was also the site of one of the city's largest evangelical churches. A showdown was imminent.

It was impossible for the believers to ignore their risqué neighbours. Every night, clients formed queues at the front doors of the brothels. Customers were mostly soldiers, miners, and truck drivers, mostly drunk. Sometimes they caroused with the harlots on the street. Fights broke out between the men. Some fights led to the use of guns. Sometimes the prostitutes themselves traded punches with clients. Brothel patrons quickly learned that their evangelical neighbours disapproved of such behaviour. Some believers paused on their way to church to deliver pavement sermons, condemning the debauchery and warning of God's judgement. Their harangues embarrassed the prostitutes, who retaliated with crude jokes against the believers. A favourite taunt was to snatch an unsuspecting churchgoer's hat as he passed the brothel door and toss it inside. 'Would you like your hat, sir?' a harlot would tease, holding it in her hands. 'Come and get it, then.' The unfortunate man would invariably walk away bareheaded, preferring to forfeit his hat rather than his reputation.

There was one person, however, whom the prostitutes never teased. When Julia Colque left her home for the short walk to church, she never feared losing her hat. No one touched it. Drunken soldiers stopped their bawdy play and the prostitutes disappeared from the streets as Julia made her way to the chapel.

Although Julia and Florencio enjoyed immunity from personal attacks, the houses were a blight on their lives. Their three sons, now adolescents, often witnessed scandal literally in their own backyard. One morning at 3 a.m., Abel was awakened by loud shouts and screams. He looked out of his bedroom window to see a man climb over the wall from the brothel next door and disappear into the shadows behind the Colque house. A few moments later, loud pounding on the family's front gate awakened Florencio and Julia. It was the police. The officers explained that a prostitute had quarrelled with one of her clients. The man had attacked and seriously injured her. The madam called the police but before they could arrive, the assailant escaped over the wall. Had the Colques seen anything that might help the lawmen apprehend him? Abel, who had been listening to this conversation from upstairs, said that he had seen a man enter their courtyard and run toward the back fence. The officers had a look and found the criminal hiding in the Colques' outhouse. As they dragged him off to jail, the man cursed Florencio and his family for betraying him. In thick, drunken accents he vowed to return as soon as he was released from custody and avenge their treachery.

The Colque brothers were not the only teenagers at risk because of the houses. One Saturday night, a friend of the boys arrived early at the church for a youth meeting. He lingered on the street talking with other young people from the church as they waited for the meeting to begin. A passing policeman saw him there and concluded that he was waiting his turn at the brothel. The officer arrested the youth on charges of immoral behaviour on the part of a minor. As the policeman was leading him away up the street, word of the arrest reached Julia Colque next door. She hurried after the officer and pleaded with him to release the boy. 'There has been a terrible mistake,' she said. 'The lad is a believer, from a good family. He certainly had no intention of entering the brothel.' In spite of her protests, however, the officer took the young man down to the station and booked him. After spending a night in jail, the 14-year-old was released to the custody of his parents, after they paid a stiff fine for his 'misdemeanour'.

Although the police dealt with small incidents related to the prostitution, they did absolutely nothing to eliminate the sex trade from the community. Their negligence was inexcusable, since the brothels were operating illegally. City ordinances prohibited houses of prostitution in residential zones. Years before, the municipal government had designated a section of empty land on the edge of the city for the brothels, but the prostitutes complained that moving there would hurt their business. The police did nothing to force the madams to obey the ordinances. Eventually, residents of Cañada Strongest Street found out why. Oruro's ex-chief of police was part owner of two of the brothels.

* * *

Since they could not expect the police to do anything to eradicate vice from their neighbourhood, the residents of Cañada Strongest Street decided to appeal to the mayor's office. A committee of representatives from the Church of God sought an audience with the mayor to ask him to remove the brothels. A log was kept of their attempt to enlist the support of the city's chief executive.

The honourable mayor of Oruro made an appointment with the representatives of the Church of God for 9 a.m. on Monday 11 April. Emilio Perez, Nicolas Rodriguez, Erasmo Estevez and Julia Colque were present at the appointed hour. The mayor did not arrive. The appointment was rescheduled for 6 p.m., the same day.

The representatives of the church returned at six o'clock as requested. The mayor did not arrive. The mayor's secretary rescheduled the meeting for Wednesday 13 April, and told the representatives they would be advised of the hour.

No one advised the representatives of the hour of the meeting. When they presented themselves at city hall, the secretary told them the meeting had been re-scheduled for Monday 18 April, at 4.30 p.m.

Representatives of the church were finally able to meet with the mayor at the indicated time. After hearing their grievance, the mayor promised he would do all within his power to remove the houses of prostitution from the city. However, he cautioned that the process would take some time.

The houses were not removed and in September the mayor of Oruro was replaced. Julia Colque made an appointment with the new mayor for 4 November, at 3 p.m. Fifteen Cañada Strongest Street residents and members of the Church of God were present at the appointed hour. They group was still waiting to see the mayor at 5 p.m., when several of the representatives had to return home. At 6 p.m. permission was finally granted to enter the mayor's office. Of the original delegation, only Julia Colque, Adrian Padilla and Erasmo Estevez remained. The mayor commented, 'Are these all the citizens who oppose the houses?' and chided the three for exaggerating the problem. Erasmo Estevez, a long-time resident of Cañada Strongest Street, countered the mayor's claim of exaggeration with evidence that the brothels presented a serious threat to public safety. His own son, Estevez said, had been murdered in a brawl that erupted in one of the houses. The mayor admitted that the bordellos were illegal, in fact, and promised to do everything within his power to remove them from the city. He mentioned that the municipality had designated land on the edge of town as a sex-trade zone and would demand that Doña Consuelo's house and the two other brothels move there. However, he indicated the process would take some time.

The houses of prostitution were still operating on Cañada Strongest Street months after the mayor promised the residents' committee to close them down. Julia Colque went to city hall to ask for another appointment with the mayor. His secretary, by now well acquainted with Señora Colque and her grievance, took her aside and asked a confidential question.

'How much money do you have for closing those houses?'

'What do you mean?' Julia asked.

'I mean the only way you are going to get rid of those places is to spend money, a lot of money. Every month the madams bring the mayor a "tip" for allowing them to operate. I don't know how much they give him, but it's a sizeable stack of bills. Can you people outspend the prostitutes? It's your only hope.'

Julia did not know what to say. She thanked the woman for the information and went home to explain to her neighbours what she had learned. They decided to raise as much money as they could from the community to fight the brothels. They also decided that instead of bribing the mayor, they would use the money to hire a lawyer. Someone suggested a Dr Miranda, pointing out that the attorney attended an evangelical church. Everybody agreed he would be their best ally since he was a brother in the faith. They went to see Dr Miranda at first opportunity.

'I will have those houses closed down within two months,' Miranda promised them. 'Leave everything to me.' He only asked that the believers pay him in advance for his services. Two months later a hearing was called in Oruro Circuit Court to hear complaints against the brothels in Cañada Strongest Street. A petition was presented calling for the immediate removal of the brothels, in accordance with city ordinances. The document was signed by Dr Miranda, counsel for the plaintiffs. Then another petition was presented calling for tolerance of the houses of prostitution. The second document requested that the court allow the prostitutes to continue operating in Cañada Strongest Street until such time as they could move their business to a suitable, alternative site. This paper was also signed by Dr Miranda, counsel for the defendants.

The believers were shocked. The same lawyer they had contracted to prosecute the case against the prostitutes was also defending them. Their shock turned to disappointment when the court ruled to accept *both* petitions. The ruling meant the houses could continue operating until such a time as the prostitutes themselves decided it would be convenient for them to move. The residents of Cañada Strongest Street realized that their savvy opponents had outmanoeuvered them. When brothel owners learned that the resident's committee had retained the services of Dr Miranda to close down their businesses, they went to him and offered a tidy sum to act in their defence. Miranda accepted their case and their money. Professional ethics, of course, prevent lawyers from representing conflicting interests in the same legal case. But in some cases, professional ethics can be ignored, for a price.

* * *

When their repeated appeals to the legal system failed to dislodge the prostitutes, the Cañada Strongest Street residents decided to turn to the press. Articles about the brothels appeared in the Oruro paper. Local radio stations broadcast news reports on the vice operations. Public exposure had its intended effect. On Thursday 16 May, 1985, a hearing was held in the Church of God chapel. The district attorney, the city supervisor, the city clerk and a circuit court judge were present to hear charges against the prostitutes. By 7.30 p.m. that evening, activity at the brothels was in full swing. Long lines of clients formed at the doors, music blared from loud speakers and drunken men traded bawdy jokes while waiting their turn with the women.

But by 9.45 p.m., the hour appointed for the hearing, everything was eerily quiet in Cañada Strongest Street. Drunks were gone from the street and the loud speakers had fallen silent. The prostitutes themselves had abandoned the houses with all their personal belongings to spend the night in other locations. The believers ushered the city officials into the chapel. The three madams who managed the brothels arrived, accompanied by their lawyer. Julia Colque recognized him as the former mayor of Oruro who had promised to do everything within his power to close down the sex trade on Cañada Strongest Street. The meeting began and the prostitutes' legal counsel addressed the panel of city officials.

'Honourable officials of the city of Oruro,' he began, 'on behalf of my clients, I would like to apologize to you for the inconvenience this meeting has caused your worthy persons. Secondly, I would like to speak on behalf of these fine ladies.' He indicated the madams, who were seated together on a front pew. 'They are the unfortunate victims of vicious slander and gossip. Certain persons, for reasons known only to themselves, have insinuated that my clients are running businesses that encourage drunkenness, disturb the peace and profit from immoral behaviour. But as your honours can see for yourselves, none of this kind of behaviour is going on here tonight. I appeal to you to disregard the unfair demand of a few cranks. Your honours must not order the closure of my clients' businesses.'

Florencio Colque tried hard to conceal his anger as he responded to the lawyer's remarks. 'Honourable officials, if you had been here earlier this evening, you would have seen with your own eyes the public disturbances and immoral behaviour that we have brought to your attention. It is clear that someone warned the prostitutes about this hearing tonight so that they could deceive you.'

Florencio sensed that a valuable opportunity to expose the scandal was slipping away. He looked around the room at his fellow believers seated in the pews and realized that few of them would dare speak before the city officials. The majority spoke Spanish poorly, many spoke no Spanish at all. The lawyer had intimidated them with his pompous speech. For an awful moment, Florencio thought he was the only one present willing to testify against the houses of prostitution. Then the district attorney broke the silence to address his colleagues on the panel. 'Señor Colque is right, gentlemen,' he said. 'We are being deceived. We all know, both from news reports and eye witness testimony that prostitution is openly practised in this neighbourhood.'

Florencio sighed with relief. The panel members conferred among themselves. After a few moments, they announced to the assembly their conclusion that the vice problem on Cañada Strongest Street was indeed serious. The situation should be rectified, they said. Unfortunately, they themselves had no authority to do anything about it.

Florencio was not satisfied with their answer. 'If your honours have no authority to close the houses, then who does?' he pressed. 'If we can't receive justice here in Oruro, then where do we go? To La Paz?'

His question was mildly threatening. The city officials shifted uneasily in their chairs. They had not expected a challenge.

'We have made inquiries in government offices in the capital,' Florencio continued. 'People there have assured us that we have the right to take this matter before the Minister of Justice, if we feel we must.'

Once again the city officials conferred among themselves. They agreed that, under the circumstances, it would be unwise to trouble the Minister of Justice about this matter. Prudence demanded that prostitution in Oruro remain a local problem, under local jurisdiction. For that reason, they said, they were prepared to rule on the question of the brothels. However, the residents must understand that any decision of the panel would be 'provisional'.

Then the officials announced their ruling. The houses must close within 90 days. A notice was to be posted in the entrance to each brothel informing the public of the closures. The meeting adjourned and the believers went home to savour their hard-won victory.

Florencio and Julia Colque had been living for years with houses of prostitution on either side of their home and another directly across the street. The family waited anxiously for the three-month period to conclude so that they would be rid of the blight. That was why they were shocked when, on the day the brothels were to close, city officials extended the closure order. The prostitutes had an extra 90 days to continue their operations on Cañada Strongest Street. This news awakened suspicion in both Florencio and Julia that worse tidings were in store. Sure enough, when the second 90-day period elapsed, city officials granted the brothels another extension, this one for 'an indefinite period'. The harlots had won again.

The Colques had exhausted every human resource available in trying to rid their community of prostitution. Even though the law was clearly on their side, civil authorities refused to see justice done. Florencio knew the only recourse now was to appeal to a higher authority. He called the family together around the dining-room table and explained his plan. 'Our only hope to remove the prostitutes is prayer. We are going to hold a family prayer vigil. I will begin, then Julia will continue after me. Then it will be Jonás's turn, then Abel's, then Javier's. We will pray until God answers us. I have no idea what the answer will be. But I am sure of this. Either the prostitutes go, or we do.'

The family agreed to follow the plan. One room of the house was set aside for the vigil and each night the Colques took their turns praying. Two weeks later, their prayers were answered.

* * *

Saul Vedia Daza, recently appointed district attorney for the Circuit Court of Oruro, went to a football match one Sunday afternoon at the municipal stadium. The stadium is sited two blocks from Cañada Strongest Street. Vedia did not own a car and planned to take a city bus home after the match. That day, however, football attracted so many fans to the stadium that all the buses were full, so the young district attorney started home on foot. Vedia was walking along Cañada Strongest Street when he noticed a crowd of people milling around on the pavement. They appeared to be having a party. As he walked past the group, he realized what type of party it was. A young woman, immodestly dressed and obviously under the influence of alcohol, was offering sexual favours to the men gathered on the street. Dr Vedia frowned at the distasteful scene. When he noticed that the prostitute was standing practically in the door of a church, distaste turned to disgust. How could vice be openly practised so close to a house of prayer? The bizarre scene aroused Vedia's suspicion.

When he arrived at his office the next day, he began to investigate the legal situation on Cañada Strongest Street. His findings confirmed his suspicions. The brothels were operating in a restricted residential zone in violation of city ordinances. As a member of the federal judiciary, Dr Vedia was authorized to compel local officials to enforce the law. He acted immediately. On Tuesday, the transcript of his legal order appeared in the local newspaper. The order stated that, in compliance with city laws, the mayor of Oruro was to proceed at once with the removal of the houses of prostitution operating in Cañada Strongest Street. Furthermore, the city was to conclude the relocation of the brothels within a period of 30 days. The decree was irrevocable and not subject to extension. It was signed by Saul Vedia Daza, District Attorney, Circuit Court of Oruro.

Florencio and Julia Colque could hardly believe their eyes when they read the newspaper notice. They read through the district attorney's order several times in order to assure themselves that it was directed at the brothels on Cañada Strongest Street, the same ones surrounding their home. Even then, they dared not believe that the prostitutes were really leaving. To date, none of the legal rulings against the houses had been enforced. This might turn out to be another phony decree. Their doubts were dispelled, however, 30 days later. The brothels closed for good. The young harlots left Cañada Strongest Street, suitcases in hand, never to be seen there again. The long queues of soldiers, miners and truck drivers did not form on the pavements that night. Nor did the loud speakers blare bawdy music into the wee hours of the morning.

As soon as he was able, Florencio went to visit Saul Vedia. The young district attorney listened with interest as Florencio recounted the community's long struggle against the prostitutes. On behalf of the church and community residents, Florencio thanked Dr Vedia for ridding them of the vice operations.

'Thank you very much for telling me this, Señor Colque,' the young attorney said quietly. 'I appreciate your support because, frankly, I seem to have put myself in a dangerous position. The day my order appeared in the newspaper, the madams came to offer me a bribe. I had expected them to try that, but I had not expected them to come up with so much money. They had a suitcase full. Enough to buy a couple of automobiles.'

Dr Vedia paused, recalling his encounter with the madams. Their enticement had been especially poignant, considering the fact that he had originally discovered the illegal brothels while walking home from the football match. If he owned a car, he would not have been walking that day.

Florencio could appreciate the temptation the young district attorney faced. 'What did you do, doctor?' he asked gently.

'I told them that attempting to bribe a public official was against the law,' Vedia replied. 'I said that if they persisted in the attempt, I would have them arrested. That made the madams angry. They said that I had better be careful, that it wouldn't surprise them if something dreadful happened to me very soon.'

'Do you think the threat was serious?' Florencio asked.

'Yes, I do. A couple of days afterward, someone called my house, threatening to kill me. I was not home at the time and my elderly mother answered the phone. She didn't know anything about the prostitution affair and it upset her badly. I requested 24-hour police protection for my house, just in case.'

The two men were silent for a moment. Florencio said solemnly, 'Do not be concerned, Dr Vedia, about their threats. God is great, much greater than our enemies. I and the believers of my church will pray that he will protect you from this danger. Nothing will happen to you, I can assure you of that.'

'Thank you,' the young lawyer said. Florencio stood to leave and the two men shook hands.

Florencio was true to his word. Now in their daily prayer vigils, he and his family interceded for Saul Vedia Daza, asking God to protect him from those who wanted to do him harm. God answered their prayers. Saul Vedia received no more threatening phone calls. Nor did anyone attempt to kill him.

His order finally and permanently evicted the prostitutes from Cañada Strongest Street. They had occupied the neighbourhood for nearly 40 years in defiance of law, community pressure and public opinion. But in the end, the centres of corruption were defeated by two forces against which they were utterly impotent: Saul Vedia's honesty and Florencio Colque's prayers.

The Final Song

Nearly four decades have passed since Florencio Colque first confessed faith in Jesus Christ. The years have brought achievement and disappointment, happiness and grief. Most of all, the years have brought change. Florencio was thinking about the changes one day when he went to work. It was a Monday morning and he was still recuperating from a long weekend of travel and preaching. The travel had been hard but well worth the opportunity it provided to teach the Bible to an attentive crowd of *campesinos*. He had chosen John 10, the Good Shepherd passage, as the basis of his Sunday morning message.

'We learned from our grandfathers to walk a certain road,' he told the congregation in Quechua. 'They told us "You must worship this well, this rock, this mountain peak." When we asked them why this was, they said, "Because this is the teaching we have received from our grandfathers." Then the priests came. They said we must stop worshipping the land and believe the gospel. But the priests spoke only in Latin and we could not understand what the gospel was.'

'Finally, humble men like ourselves came to us with the gospel. They spoke to us in our own language, so that we could understand and believe. Now we have come out of the darkness, we have entered the light. Now we worship God in spirit and in truth.'

'When I was a boy, I called my sheep,' he concluded. '"Baaa! Baaa!" I called and they listened. When they were certain it was me calling, they followed because they recognized my voice. In the same way we, like sheep, must learn to recognize Jesus' voice from all the others and follow him.' When Florencio finished preaching, a few of the listeners came to him and expressed their desire to follow Jesus. Later, he helped local elders baptize the new converts. Florencio never tired of performing that particular task.

He climbed onto the road grader, fired up the engine and pointed the big machine down the road. His thoughts turned to his family back in town. At that moment, Julia would be leaving for the station to catch the bus to La Paz. She needed to get an early start in order to be home the same night with fabric to make a wedding dress. A young couple getting married in the church next weekend had asked Florencio and Julia to be their godparents. Before Julia left for La Paz, however, she would send their three sons off to school. Florencio and Julia were proud of their sons. All were above-average students and planned to enter university following graduation from secondary school. Jonás would eventually complete post-graduate degrees in engineering in Belgium, Abel would study business administration in Mexico and Javier economy at the Technical University of Oruro. Florencio thought of his own limited days in the classroom and of his father, who had never learned to read. He smiled to himself. In only two generations, the Colques had risen from illiteracy to university.

Florencio came to the section of roadway that the foreman had assigned him and lowered the blade of the road grader. The machine shuddered as the steel bit into the gravel. The diesel engine throttled back, labouring as the grader ploughed rocks and dirt before it. Florencio felt the familiar thrill of being in control of the powerful machine. He was pleased to have this job.

The foreman was pleased with his job, as well. 'You men need to watch Florencio and learn from him,' the boss told new hires. 'He's one of the best men we've got. He's honest, he works hard and he doesn't drink. You have to respect a man like that, even if you don't believe the same things he does.'

Florencio had worked hard to earn respect. He recalled the times, years before as a boy in Lequepalca, when his playmates ridiculed him for being an orphan. Now those same playmates begged him, year after year, to run for town mayor. Florencio consistently refused the post because he was too busy with church work. He would have thought it necessary to discharge his civic duty, except that the rest of the candidates for mayor were Christians, as well. Lequepalca had become, for all practical purposes, an evangelical town. Taverns sold little *chicha* these days. Disputes over land and water rights were as likely to be settled before the deacons of the church than before the town council.

The road grader hit a stretch of gravel that had been worn into gentle undulations by the pounding of heavy trucks. The grinding of the steel blade on the corrugated road surface settled into a steady throb. The sound echoed in Florencio's head and set his foot to tapping. The rhythm, not unlike the metre of folk hymns he customarily sang in church, inspired him to compose a song. Its words, like those of the songs sung by Florencio's ancient forebear, Pachacutec, were Quechua. Its theme was the same that inspired Inca poets to compose hymns to Viracocha. And yet, Florencio's simple song was notably different from the ancient ballads. Pachacutec, notwithstanding his hunger to discover the Creator of the world, had only the evidence of nature at hand to reveal God's greatness. But Florencio had come to know God in person, through the witness of the Spirit and the Word.

That night when he returned to the road camp, Florencio wrote down the words of his song on a slip of paper. Some months later, a man heard the tune and asked Florencio to sing it into a tape recorder. The man later transcribed the song and published it in a Quechua hymnbook. From then on, Christian believers across Bolivia would sing Florencio's song at church meetings and *juntas*.

'I Will Testify'

Testimonioywan	With a true testimony,
Dios chimpaykamuyki	I want to draw near, God.
Yachaspa cruzpi	Knowing that, on the cross,
Qan wañusqaykita	You have died.
Testimonioywan	With a true testimony,
Dios qayilaykamuyki	Closer I will draw near.
Creespa Qanlla	Believing that you
Salvawasqaykita	Have given me salvation.
Testimonioywan	With a true testimony,
Dios Qanman jamuyku	I have come before you, God.
Churiykimin	Your Son
Juchaykuta mayllarqa	Washed me of my sin.

-The End-

Bibliography

Andrade, Victor, *My Missions For Revolutionary Bolivia,* Pittsburgh: University of Pittsburgh Press, 1976.

Arguedes, Alcides, *Historia General de Bolivia*, La Paz: Gisbert & Cia., 1975.

Barton, Robert, *A Short History of the Republic of Bolivia*, La Paz: Los Amigos del Libro, 1968.

del Busto, José Antonio, *Compendio de Historia del Peru*, Lima: Studium, 1983.

Firestone, Homer, *The Andean Soul*, Cochabamba: Mobile, 1984.

Firestone, Homer, *The Gospel According to Bolivia*, Cochabamba: Mobile, 1984.

Klein, Herbert S., *Bolivia: The Evolution of a Multi-Ethnic Society*, Oxford: Oxford University Press, 1982.

Lanning, Edward P., *Peru Before the Incas*, Englewood Cliffs: Prentice-Hall, 1967.

Lara, Jesús, *La Cultura de los Incas*, second edition, Cochabamba: Los Amigos del Libro, 1975.

Richardson, Don, *Eternity in Their Hearts*, Ventura, CA: Regal, 1981.

Schoop, Wolfgang, *Ciudades Bolvianas*, La Paz: Los Amigos del Libro, 1981.

Wolf, Eric R., *Europe and the People Without History*, London: University of California Press, 1982.